HIRING THE BEST PERSON

FOR EVERY JOB

PARTICIPANT WORKBOOK

HIRING THE BEST PERSON
FOR EVERY JOB

DeANNE ROSENBERG

JOSSEY-BASS/PFEIFFER
A Wiley Company
www.pfeiffer.com

Published by
JOSSEY-BASS/PFEIFFER
A Wiley Company
989 Market Street
San Francisco, CA 94103-1741
415.433.1740; Fax 415.433.0499
800.274.4434; Fax 800.569.0443

www.pfeiffer.com

ISBN: 0-7879-5897-2

Acquiring Editor: Josh Blatter
Director of Development: Kathleen Dolan Davies
Developmental Editor: Susan Rachmeler
Editor: Rebecca Taff
Senior Production Editor: Dawn Kilgore
Manufacturing Supervisor: Becky Carreño
Cover Design: Bruce Lundquist and Chris Wallace
Illustrations: Lotus Art

Printing 10 9 8 7 6 5 4 3 2 1

CONTENTS

INTRODUCTION TO THE WORKSHOP

WELCOME TO THIS INTERVIEWING WORKSHOP that will present you with a very innovative approach to interviewing. The strategy you will learn makes minimal use of the candidate's resume. Moreover, it does not rely on human resources to provide you with a job description and competencies (which are probably out of date anyway). This workshop will guide you through a process of meticulous preparation based on your performance expectations. This will be followed by a discussion of the many different questioning tactics for interviewing. You will learn about insightful listening, including the reading of body language cues so that, at the end, you will have a "no fail" strategy for selecting the best person for every job.

Interviewing is a skill. The only way to learn a skill is through practice. Therefore this workshop will involve considerable role-play activity. Others who have been through this workshop have truly enjoyed themselves, so please sit back, relax, and prepare to have an enjoyable learning experience.

Workshop Objectives

By the end of this workshop, you will be able to

- Design a strategy for a more targeted approach to the interview based on the *Master Match Matrix*®;
- Make a decision about a candidate's strengths and weaknesses within 40 minutes;
- Develop effective question-generation techniques based on specific job objectives;
- Utilize a variety of questioning techniques to be used during interviews;

- Match candidate and questioning technique for maximum data collection;

- Separate listening from evaluation during the interview process;

- Use active listening techniques;

- Understand and "read" the hidden meanings in body language;

- Utilize two theoretical approaches to interviewing: (1) Interviewing by Objectives and (2) McClelland's Theory of Personality Fit, known as People Reading; and

- Recognize the Equal Opportunity restrictions and discuss their implications for the interview process.

You will leave this workshop with your own, individually developed, Master Match Matrix® that you will be able to use whenever you interview for the particular position that you've selected.

Interviewing Quiz

Directions: How much do you really know about interviewing? While you are waiting for this workshop to begin, why not test yourself and see by circling **T** for **true** or **F** for **false** after each question below. It will take about 10 minutes. The answers are on pages A-7–A-9 of this workbook.

1. Most interviews are unreliable because they are performed in a biased fashion.   T   F

2. A truly skilled interviewer will be completely objective.   T   F

3. Characteristics that impress interviewers favorably include verbal facility, a neat appearance, cordiality, and conformity.   T   F

4. Basically, interviewing behavior and attitude are similar to the job behavior and attitude; therefore, if you can accurately assess the one, you will have also accurately assessed the other.   T   F

5. Interviewing is a necessary function of management, but it does not relate to the economic success of the company.   T   F

6. Hiring decisions are usually based on feelings rather than on facts; on the relationship that develops between the interviewer and the candidate, rather than on the requirements of the job.   T   F

7. Managers tend to hire in their own image, that is, people who are like them in background, experience, attitude, opinions, and even looks.   T   F

8. Candidates who are unemployed at the time of the interview are considered just as desirable as those who are employed at the time of the interview.   T   F

9. Generally, interviewers appreciate candidates with unusual backgrounds, nontraditional experience, and individualistic ideas that do not necessarily coincide with those of the interviewer.   T   F

10. Stress interviews are an effective way to determine the candidate's ability to deal with job-related stress.   T   F

11. In a good interview, the candidate should do 80 percent of the talking.   T   F

12. The interviewer is responsible for (reducing the anxiety) settling the applicant down. The applicant is responsible for maintaining a free-flowing discussion.   T   F

13. The interview should give you all the information you need to make the hiring decision.   T   F

14. It is important to evaluate as you progress through the interview.   T F

15. A competent interviewer ignores his or her intuition (gut feelings) in making the hiring decision.   T F

16. The best time to evaluate a candidate is two or three days after the interview, when you've had a chance to really mull things over.   T F

17. Your company is responsible for any EEO (Equal Employment Opportunity) errors you may make in interviewing.   T F

18. Promotability should always be a consideration in selecting a candidate.   T F

19. Evaluation should be kept separate from the data-gathering portion of the interview.   T F

20. You can ask marriage and family-related or personal questions of your candidates without violating EEO legislation.   T F

21. The way in which you ask a question will influence the answer you receive.   T F

22. Most hiring decisions are made in the first 4 minutes of the interview (first impressions are virtually impossible to change).   T F

23. The most important skill in interviewing is listening.   T F

24. A "good" candidate should volunteer personal information without your having to probe for it.   T F

25. The interview does not really measure what people claim it is supposed to measure: competence, commitment, and ability to work well with others.   T F

Cost of Turnover

U.S. Department of Labor statistics indicate that 40 percent of all new hires leave within the first six months and 50 percent of all management-level candidates fail in their new positions within their first six months on the job. Some leave because the job does not meet their expectations; others are asked to leave because they prove to be incompetent. At an average salary of $45,000/year, companies are throwing away vast sums of money on hiring errors that could be easily eliminated with training in preparation and the use of a perceptive, logical, and repeatable system. The information shown below is based on an employee salary of $45,000 a year.

1.	Cost of inadequacy of the new employee (12 months)	$20,800
2.	Cost of assistance by peers and staff closely associated with the new employee	$14,350
3.	Cost of declining productivity of departing employee	$ 2,600
4.	Cost of shift of attention from the work to the departing employee by peers and staff	$ 900
5.	Cost of leaving the position vacant or functioning with stopgap measures (13 weeks)	$21,750
6.	Cost of processing both the departing employee and the new employee by HR	$ 1,085
7.	Cost of recruitment (newspaper ads, agency fees, etc.) and screening of applicants by HR	$ 2,890
8.	Cost of supervisor/manager's time in orienting and training the new employee	$ 2,930
9.	Cost of relocation	0
	Total Cost	**$67,305**
	Ratio of Costs to Average Salary	**1.55%**

Source: The categories and percentages are based on a 1990 study done by the Society for Human Resource Management and published in the December 1990 issue of *Personnel Journal*; financial data is based on 2000 salary figures.

INTERVIEWING BY OBJECTIVES AND USING THE MASTER MATCH MATRIX®

Discussion Notes

Use the following outline of the topic to take notes as your facilitator leads you through the material. Various exercises are also provided for you to complete, as directed by your facilitator.

Victimization of the Untrained Interviewer

1. Experience

2. Education

3. Verbal agility

Four Criteria Traditionally Used for Selection

1. Personal preferences of the interviewer

2. Personality traits and aptitude of the applicant

3. Educational background of the applicant

4. Behavioral skills of the applicant

Investigative Questions

1. What would you do if. . .?

2. What has been your experience with. . .?

3. What has been the most challenging. . .?

Puzzle Questions Versus Behavioral Questions

Exercise 1

REWORKING PUZZLE AND BEHAVIORAL QUESTIONS

Directions: Please rewrite the following questions. If they are puzzle questions, make them behavioral; if they are behavioral, make them puzzle questions. *Suggested Time:* 5 minutes. The answers are provided on pages A-9–A-10 of this workbook.

1. Tell me about a time when you coached an employee about his or her lack of attention to detail.

2. What have you done to ensure that your staff members freely share information with one another?

3. What would you do if your manager asked you for feedback on a peer's performance?

4. When changes are imminent, how far in advance have you informed your staff?

5. What would you do about an employee who had problems identifying his or her priorities?

6. Describe a conflict situation where you played the role of mediator.

7. Suppose your manager wanted you to terminate an employee and you thought the person might be saved with some solid coaching efforts. What would you do?

8. How can a manager ensure objectivity when giving performance feedback to an annoying and difficult staff member?

9. Tell me about a time when you stepped outside the boundaries of your experience and knowledge to solve a serious problem.

10. Give me an example of unethical behavior in the workplace.

11. What are the critical qualities of a good manager?

12. What has been your experience with coaching risk taking in others?

The Fifth Criterion: Selection by Objectives

- Concerned with the candidate's past record of results
- Interviewer compares *past performance* against the *job objectives* of the vacancy and the manager's *expectations* for the candidate's performance
- Job description versus job objectives

  Job description just lists activities to be performed

  Job objectives identify results, outputs, deliverables, achievements, and performance expectations

PERFORMANCE EXPECTATIONS WORKSHEET

What expectations, when fulfilled, will I regard as satisfactory performance?

Position Title:

The key responsibilities for this position are . . .	The performance level that I will consider satisfactory is . . .	This is how I will measure performance:	Based on my expectations and the performance I expect, the candidate will need these competencies:

COMPETENCIES REQUIRED WORKSHEET

What a Person MUST Have, Know, or Be Able to Do in Order to Do this Job Successfully

Every position requires certain abilities, knowledge, and skills that the candidate *must* have in order to be successful in that job. Before starting the interview process, it is critical that you know the competencies or factors that have been determined to be the keys to the success of others who have held this particular job. In the space below, please list the competencies in this job vacancy that will ensure a person's success in this position.

Job Vacancy Title: _____

Competencies Required:

1.

2.

3.

4.

5.

6.

7.

8.

The Screening Process

- No candidate will measure up in all respects

- Must be able to evaluate tradeoffs

- As a buyer of services, think in terms of output desired

The Master Match Matrix®

Three steps:

1. Identify the competencies desired and weight each according to priority

2. Refine your terms by clarifying exactly what you mean by each competency. For example: In order to interview successfully, think about what you mean in a very specific way. Suppose one of your competencies is "good communicator."

    Do you mean verbally or in writing?

    Do you mean communicate with various levels in the organization?

    Do you mean communicate with customers, suppliers, and vendors?

    Do you mean communicate with people from different cultures, with people for whom English is not their primary language?

    Do you mean communicate face-to-face?

    Do you mean communicate on the telephone?

    Do you mean communicate through correspondence via letters, written reports, or by e-mail?

3. Generate questions to determine whether candidate has necessary competencies.

MASTER MATCH MATRIX®

POSITION: _____

Candidate's Name:	first priority competency	second priority competency	third priority competency	fourth priority competency	fifth priority competency	sixth priority competency	seventh priority competency	eighth priority competency	Total score:

Needs → ← Wants

SAMPLE MASTER MATCH MATRIX®

POSITION: Administrative Manager

Candidate's Name:	Needs					Wants			Total score:
	Two years' experience supervising	Delegation & coaching skills	Participative leadership style	Conflict management skills	Goal settings as a management strategy	Superior communication skills	College graduate	Professional appearance	
Agnes Jones	8	3	2	1	0	1	0	0	15
Phil Aline	7.5	5	6	5	2	2	1	1	29.5
Joseph Potter	8	6	6	5	2	1	2	1	31
Hannah Spolling	8	3	5	5	2	3	1	0	27
Louise Baker	4	7	6	3	2	3	2	1	28
Connie DeLessie	7.5	7	6	5	4	3	2	0	34.5
Oscar Lemoninen	4	7	3	2	0	1	2	1	20

COMPLETING THE MASTER MATCH MATRIX®

Look at the sample MMM® that has been completed for you on the previous page before continuing. Setting up and completing the blank Master Match Matrix® that has been provided for any job opening (page 9) is a three-step process. First, describe, in broad brush strokes, the various skills, competencies, knowledge, experience, and qualities that you are seeking in the candidate.

Second, paint as clear a picture as possible of those qualities you seek.

Third, select and frame the exact questions you intend to put to the candidate in the actual interview.

It is important to remember that you can put anything you want on the MMM®—as long as you have a way of scoring it that satisfies you. Some items, if described specifically enough (such as three years' experience as a foreman in a unionized manufacturing setting), are easy to score. Other items (such as punctuality, ability to get along with others, and so forth) are not at all easy to quantify. For these kinds of items, you need to provide some additional descriptive information to clarify, in your own mind, exactly what you are looking for.

On the pages that follow, you will find a selection of possible competencies, along with more specific meanings and interview questions.

Step One: Competency: MOTIVATION

Step Two: BASIC MEANINGS

- Interest in this type of work
- Works with minimum of supervision
- Willing to go beyond what's in the job description
- Interested in becoming better at what he or she is doing (self-development)

Step Three: QUESTIONS TO ASK DURING THE INTERVIEW

- "What are the three major reasons why you are considering leaving your present job?"
- "If hired, what would you want to be doing in this job in six months? How about in one year?"
- "How much of a management role do you like in order to produce good results?"

- "How do you get support for the things you want to do?"

- "Tell me about any special assignments you handled that were outside your regular responsibilities."

- "What situations have you faced where additional responsibilities were thrust on you unexpectedly?"

- "How much of your own time and/or money have you spent on your own personal development in the past twelve months, and for what specific reasons?"

- "What have you done recently to become more effective in your present job?"

Step One: Competency: GOOD HUMAN RELATIONS

Step Two: BASIC MEANINGS

- Gets along well with co-workers
- Cooperates when asked
- Helps others without being asked
- Good with customers
- Even-tempered; has self-control

Step Three: QUESTIONS TO ASK DURING THE INTERVIEW

- "If you were teaching a course in human relations on the job and you could cover only two points, what would you cover?"

- "What would you say is your preferred technique for dealing with people at work?"

- "What kinds of things frustrate you the most at work? How do you deal with them?"

- "Describe the qualities in people whom you have found most difficult for others to deal with."

- "How have you handled things when you could see the light at the end of the tunnel and the organization suddenly gave you more tunnel?"

- "Suppose you were in the middle of a project and the organization required your expertise on another assignment. How would you go about leaving the first project so that another person could take it up where you left off?"

- "What has been your experience dealing with irate customers?"
- "In a situation where you need cooperation from peers, how do you ensure their support for the things you want to do?"

Step One: Competency: TEAM PLAYER

Step Two: BASIC MEANINGS

- Interacts well with others
- Exhibits excellent listening and communication skills
- Is willing to do more than his or her "fair share"
- Knows how and when to compromise and negotiate
- Is able and willing to resolve conflicts with teammates

Step Three: QUESTIONS TO ASK DURING THE INTERVIEW

- "What has been your experience working on a team as a team member?"
- "What was the most difficult situation you faced as a team member? How was that situation resolved?"
- "What role did you play in that situation?"
- "Describe the circumstances under which you would work most effectively on a team."
- "What is your idea of a good 'team player'?"
- "What are the major differences between being an effective employee and being an effective team member?"
- "What do you think a team should do when one member does not carry his or her own weight?"
- "From your point of view, what are the three most important things a supervisor should provide or do for his or her team?"
- "What qualities, behaviors, and attitudes should one team member expect and receive from other members?"

Step One: Competency: LEADERSHIP SKILLS

Step Two: BASIC MEANINGS

- Build and maintain collaborative working relationships with their staff
- Build and maintain an atmosphere of trust
- Manage conflict effectively
- Utilize goal setting as a motivational and productivity strategy
- Inspire each employee to stretch his or her capabilities

Step Three: QUESTIONS TO ASK DURING THE INTERVIEW

- "What have you done to maintain a strong relationship between yourself and your staff?"
- "What role have you played in managing conflicts that arise between staff members?"
- "What techniques have you used to encourage your people to give you the 'bad news' when they make mistakes?"
- "Tell me about a time when you influenced a staff member to take on a task that you knew would be difficult for him or her."
- "When you know that an employee is having a performance problem, what kind of assistance have you provided to him or her?"
- "What techniques have you used to encourage employees to develop their own capabilities?"
- "How would you motivate an employee who is afraid to make decisions?"
- "What role has goal setting played in your leadership strategy?"
- "Suppose you had an employee who set easily achieved goals; how would you encourage him or her to set more challenging goals?"

Candidates with Little or No Experience

Motivation

Note Taking

Exercise 2
QUESTION GENERATION

Directions: In the following exercise, please create a behavioral question that targets the competency indicated. (Your question should not give away the answer you are seeking.) *Suggested Time:* 10 minutes. The answers are on pages A-10–A-13 of this workbook.

1. Competency: ability to manage others effectively

2. Competency: beliefs and values are compatible with those of the organization

3. Competency: team player

4. Competency: flexible

5. Competency: good communication skills

6. Competency: ability to use his or her initiative

7. Competency: self-starter

8. Competency: good interpersonal skills

9. Competency: good decision maker

10. Competency: ability to sell; salesmanship

11. Competency: customer service focus

12. Competency: emotional maturity

Benefits of the MMM®

PRE-PLANNING THE INTERVIEW (Two-Day Format Only)

Directions: Take 30 minutes to discuss the assigned set of questions with your group.

Know Your Biases

1. How do a candidate's clothes influence your opinion of his or her skills? Are you favorably disposed toward conservative "business" dress? What about people who appear slovenly, unkempt, and disheveled?

   Comments:

2. Are you more receptive to physically attractive applicants? Is this true for both male and female candidates?

   Comments:

3. Do you often have a *good* first impression of a person and then later change your mind? Can you explain why? Do you ever have a bad impression first and then later change your mind? Why do you suppose this happens?

   Comments:

4. What kind(s) of person do you find it most difficult to interview? Why?

   Comments:

Know Your Company

5. What is the most controversial topic that an applicant might raise about your organization? How would you deal with it in an interview?

   Comments:

6. How would you describe the "personality" of your company?

   Comments:

7. How do your salaries and fringe benefits compare with others in the same field? What other good reasons are there to come to work with you?

   Comments:

8. What is your company's ranking in its field? How does this opening fit into the overall organization?

   Comments:

Know the Purposes and Pitfalls of the Interview Process

9. One of the reasons for an interview is because resumes and applications generally do not provide enough information on which to base a hiring decision. What are the most common areas of information from resumes and applications that need to be clarified during the interview?

    Comments:

10. Are you convinced that a personal interview is an essential step in the employment process? List five different things you can accomplish with an interview that would be difficult or impossible to achieve without one.

    1.

    2.

    3.

    4.

    5.

11. What do you feel is the single most important thing for you to be cautious about before an interview?

    Comments:

12. What do you feel are the most common mistakes you might make in the interview? How could they be avoided?

    Comments:

Know What the Candidate Might Want to Know

13. Make believe that you are a professional person with a good track record who is casually looking around for a new opportunity in an organization closely allied to your prior experience. What are the five most important questions you would want the interviewer to answer for you?

1.

2.

3.

4.

5.

14. Now put yourself in the role of the interviewer. Considering your present knowledge of your vacancy and the company, how would you answer those questions for the candidate?

1.

2.

3.

4.

5.

How to Guarantee Superior Recruitment Assistance from HR or an Employment Agency

In most organizations today, when you discover you need to add a person to your staff, you approach HR with a requisition and a basic job description (which lists tasks and responsibilities) and ask HR to begin a recruitment process. Human resources will screen numbers of applicants and refer a "short list" of possible candidates to you. Many of those referred as viable candidates will probably be unacceptable. A good deal of time will be wasted by both you and the Human Resources Department because they really do not understand exactly what you want.

Although HR is staffed with very perceptive people, they do not know your business as intimately as you do. No matter what you tell them, there is so much more hidden information that only you have. The problem is to get that information to human resources in some sort of format that will make sense to them. The MMM® strategy will do that for you. So will the information on the following pages, which contains some of the data human resources will want to know, along with a form that you can use to submit the information to human resources.

Education/Training/Skills

Can you list these in tangible terms?

Does HR understand the relevance of those skills to the job?

Are there tradeoffs between education/experience that you would accept? Specify.

Why are these skills desired (present or future need)?

Personality Traits Sought

From you . . . from peers

How are they defined?

Are they measurable?

Can you rank as to relevance?

Can you describe accurately?

What questions should HR ask to discover their existence?

Knockout Factors (unwilling to travel, no driver's license, etc.)

Why are these disqualifying?

Any tradeoffs or substitutes?

Can HR cover these prior to your interview?

Special Qualifications Sought (experience with a given customer group, foreign language, etc.)

Does HR know why these are important?

How can HR verify them?

Specific Technical Experience

Does HR have a basic understanding of technical background needed?

Does HR know where tradeoffs/substitutes are possible?

Does HR know how this experience will be utilized?

Does HR think the requirements are realistic and obtainable?

Does HR understand what experience is especially relevant?

Does HR know whether this experience represents a present or future need?

Turnons

Does HR know what to tell the candidate about the position, department, product, or company to create interest?

Is it challenging, interesting, different, and unique?

Promotional Possibilities

Does HR know what they are in terms of responsibilities, titles, and dollars?

Compensation Package

What is the range of minimum and maximum salary figures possible?

What are the short-term benefits (two years) in dollar value?

What are the long-term benefits (over two years)?

JOB DESCRIPTION FORM

Position Title: _____   Reports To: _____

Duties _____
_____
_____
_____
_____

Knockout Factors (if any) _____
_____
_____
_____
_____

Working Conditions   Promotional Possibilities
_____   _____
_____   _____
_____   _____
_____   _____

Educational Requirements   Technical/Skill Requirements
_____   _____
_____   _____
_____   _____
_____   _____

Personality Traits Sought   Other Requirements (Experience)
_____   _____
_____   _____
_____   _____
_____   _____

TOOLS FOR INTERVIEWING

Discussion Notes

Time Frame

Courtesy Interview	20 minutes
Sell the Job	10 minutes
Second Area of Inquiry	5 minutes
Third Area of Inquiry	5 minutes

Structured Format

Structuring Statement

A brief statement that lets the candidate know what to expect

Operant Conditioning

Candidate will quickly learn the "right" way to interview based on your interviewing behavior

Questioning Strategies

Direct Questions

- Asks for a specific piece of info
- Answerable by "yes" or "no," numbers, or dates
- Limited information potential

Open-Ended Questions

- Allows for a wide range of answers
- Begins with "what," "when," "where," "who," or "why"
- Gives some insight on how the candidate thinks

Barbara Walters Technique

- Fine-tuning and refining the initial question without permitting the candidate to answer the initial question (asking multiple questions all at once)

- To be avoided because it allows the candidate to choose which question to answer

Clarifying (or Probing) Questions

- Asks for more information or a more complete response
- Two types: (1) asks for a definition or (2) asks for an illustration

Use of Clichés

Body Language Cues

- Candidate's body language is significant immediately after interviewer poses question

- Majority of message is conveyed by body language (which includes tone of voice)

- Two significant body language cues: (1) eye contact and (2) distance between parties

- Responding to body language cues

- The interviewer's body language

Self-Appraisal Questions

- Asks candidates to evaluate themselves

- Helps to discover possible negative candidate traits when used with silence

- Never say, "Tell me about your weaknesses."

Using Silence

- Silence is especially important (1) immediately after interviewer asks a question and (2) immediately after the candidate's initial response

- Allow 20 seconds after you ask question for candidate to respond

Encouragements

Listening Skills

Recognizing and responding to the candidate's context

Parrot (Echo)

Paraphrase

Feedback of Feelings

Support/Confront

- Used to reassure the candidate that what he or she just said will not harm his or her candidacy and to

- Move the conversation along quickly with a related open-ended question

Broken Record Technique

- Asking the same question again and again

- Use when candidate is being evasive

Opening and Closing the Interview

Exercise 3
RECOGNIZING TYPES OF QUESTIONS

Directions: In the space provided, identify the type of question or comment shown. *Suggested Time:* 5 minutes. Answers are provided on page A-13 of this workbook.

1. What has been the most challenging customer service situation you've had to deal with?

2. How many people were involved with you on that project?

3. Tell me what you mean by a "potentially dangerous situation."

4. What would you do if a peer questioned your integrity in front of others?

5. How often and under what circumstances would you leave written instructions for your staff?

6. What specific work experiences have done the most to prepare you for the challenges of a senior management position?

7. What would you do if you had a very talented and capable employee who continually violated the chain of command?

8. What percentage of the time were you on the road in that job?

9. What special skills would make you a valuable contributor in this job?

10. Give me an example of how you monitored that situation.

11. Good! Do go on.

12. How did you persuade the others that your idea was the way to go?

Exercise 4
TOOLS AND TECHNIQUES

Directions: Please describe the recommended use of the following tools and/or techniques in the interview process. *Suggested Time:* 5 minutes. Answers are provided on pages A-13–A-14 of this workbook.

1. Broken Record:

2. Puzzle Question:

3. Structuring Statement:

4. Behavioral Questions:

5. Self-Appraisal Question:

6. Encouragements:

7. Support/Confront:

8. Clarifying Question:

9. Open-Ended Question:

10. Barbara Walters Technique:

11. Direct Question:

12. Feedback of Feelings:

Exercise 5
READING BODY LANGUAGE

Directions: In the examples below, please interpret the candidate's body language and indicate what would be the appropriate response from the interviewer. *Suggested Time:* 10 minutes. The answers are on pages A-14–A-15 of this workbook.

1. *Interviewer:* "This organization has made it a policy not to give out signing bonuses because, upon joining the company, everyone is automatically given stock and 100 percent immediate participation in our profit-sharing plan."
   Candidate: [pushes back against the chair; crosses arms across chest; squares shoulders] "Oh, I see."

   Interpretation of body language:

   Appropriate response:

2. *Interviewer:* "We train our customer service reps to resolve all customer complaints on their own."
   Candidate: [averts eyes; looks down then looks out the window; crosses legs] "I've had lots of experience making those kinds of decisions."

   Interpretation of body language:

   Appropriate response:

3. *Interviewer:* "So what happened when you formally became the team leader?"
   Candidate: "The transition was . . . you know . . . [twists hands; looks down] ummm . . .quite a challenge."

   Interpretation of body language:

   Appropriate response:

4. *Interviewer:* "That must have been a very difficult assignment."
   Candidate: [leans forward in chair, eyes open wide, begins making hand gestures, speed of language increases] "It was more than just difficult; I was actually working on something that had never been done before—something that had been thought to be impossible."

   Interpretation of body language:

   Appropriate response:

5. *Interviewer:* "What has been your experience with teenagers as customers?"
   Candidate: [jaw gets tights, eyes avert to side, arms cross across chest] "They certainly are an interesting group as customers go."

   Interpretation of body language:

   Appropriate response:

6. *Interviewer:* "Please comment on your experience with negotiating for such things as the division of scarce resources between a number of departments, priorities between peers who report to different areas, and so on. Specific examples would be helpful."
   Candidate: [blink rate increases; eyes avert upward, hand comes to face and touches nose] "I've done a lot of that type of negotiating at previous jobs. It's kind of a part of team-based organizational life, isn't it?"

   Interpretation of body language:

   Appropriate response:

7. *Interviewer:* "What experience have you had dealing directly with customers?"
   Candidate: [presses back into the chair, leans back increasing the distance between you, crosses arms across chest] "Your newspaper ad didn't say anything about customer contact."

   Interpretation of body language:

   Appropriate response:

8. *Interviewer:* "So what occupies you when you are not working?"
   Candidate: [leans forward in chair, eyes widen, big smile, uses hands to illustrate, voice is strong and higher in pitch] "I am an active member of a regional soccer team. We travel all over the East Coast for meets and right now we are number one in the region."

   Interpretation of body language:

   Appropriate response:

9. *Interviewer:* "I'd be interested to learn what made you decide to seek another job opportunity at this point in your career."
   Candidate: [head drops down toward the floor, one hand rubs the back of the neck, head comes up, eye contact is direct, voice is weak, pace of words is slow and strained] "Well . . . I guess you could say I decided I needed to get involved with something more challenging."

   Interpretation of body language:

   Appropriate response:

10. *Interviewer:* "I can appreciate the difficulty it might create for you if we checked your references at your present employer. However, if we extend you a job offer and if you accept it, we will check those references within your first week of employment."
    Candidate: [pushes away from the desk, sits back into the chair, crosses legs and arms, jaw gets tight, eye contact is direct and hostile] "What happens if the information you receive is negative?"

    Interpretation of body language:

    Appropriate response:

11. *Interviewer:* "I'm not familiar with that type of work situation. Could you give me some specific examples so that I understand a little better?"
    Candidate: "Ummm . . . well . . . [hands flail around, eyes glance all around the room] it's kinda hard to put specifics on it. Mostly it's about using your intuition and judgment."

    Interpretation of body language:

    Appropriate response:

12. *Interviewer:* "As I understand it, you're telling me that your boss never provided you with clear goals and objectives. Is that right?"
    Candidate: "Right!" [direct eye contact, slaps fist into palm, swerves head, voice is strong]

    Interpretation of body language:

    Appropriate response:

Exercise 6
LISTENING FOR SUBSTANCE

Directions: In the following exercise, determine the real meaning of what the candidate has told you and what you should be concerned about. Then design a question that will address your concern. *Suggested Time:* 10 minutes. Suggested responses are provided on pages A-15–A-16 of this workbook.

1. "But it really wasn't my fault. My co-workers conspired to prevent me from obtaining the information I needed to do my job."

   What concerns you here?

   How will you address that concern?

2. "No one really kept track of the hours you were there. The manager only cared that the work was done right and on time."

   What concerns you here?

   How will you address that concern?

3. "I've never been good with details. I'm more of a concept person."

   What concerns you here?

   How will you address that concern?

4. "Frankly, the paperwork is a pain in the you-know-where. I'd rather be out there selling."

   What concerns you here?

   How will you address that concern?

5. "They never did pay me what I was worth, you know. But since the boss was not one to watch the expense accounts too closely, I'd get to make it up there."

What concerns you here?

How will you address that concern?

6. "My old boss may tell you that I was compulsive about details, but I just wanted to be absolutely certain that nothing was left to chance, so I created a number of forms and procedures to ensure that all the bases were covered."

What concerns you here?

How will you address that concern?

7. "I'm one person who minds her own business. Work is not a place to socialize. I sure wish others would realize that."

What concerns you here?

How will you address that concern?

8. "Clerical staff take up too much management time with their constant bickering. I prefer to work with a staff of professionals who are happy to communicate via e-mail."

What concerns you here?

How will you address that concern?

9. "I think that twelve absences per year is a reasonable expectation."
   What concerns you here?

   How will you address that concern?

10. "At my last job, I organized the Christmas party and the summer clambake. I was also the company's chief representative for the United Way collection."
    What concerns you here?

    How will you address that concern?

11. "Oh, in that job I really didn't have any experience that would pertain to this position. But I would like to discuss the job I had previous to that one."
    What concerns you here?

    How will you address that concern?

12. "I'm not a believer in close supervision and control. I like to tell my people what the goals are and let them work out the best way to achieve them."
    What concerns you here?

    How will you address that concern?

ADVANCED QUESTIONING CHALLENGES
(Two-Day Format Only)

Discussion Notes

Getting the Shy Candidate to Speak
Three methods

-

-

-

Making Questions More Productive
Four methods

-

-

-

-

Making the Interview More Conversational
Three methods

-

-

-

Dumb Questions
Four types

-

-

-

-

Responding to Evasion Tactics
Four types

-

-

-

-

Exercise 7
RESCUING DUMB QUESTIONS

Directions: The following exchanges illustrate the use of "dumb" questions. In the space provided, please rescue the dialogue so that the interview can move forward productively. *Suggested Time:* 5 minutes. The answers are provided on page A-17 of this workbook.

1. *Interviewer:* "This job requires someone who can think and make decisions quickly. How are you at decision making?"

   Candidate: "I'm very good at decision making."

2. *Interviewer:* "Are you meticulous about details or are you somewhat casual in that area?"

   Candidate: "I'm very detail-oriented."

3. *Interviewer:* "Are you a self-starter or do you need a prod now and then from the boss?"

   Candidate: "I'm a real strong self-starter."

4. *Interviewer:* "This job requires someone who can handle a lot of stress. How are you at handling stress?"

   Candidate: "Stress is no problem for me. In fact, I do my best work when I'm under stress."

5. *Interviewer:* "How well do you get along with other people?"

   Candidate: "People skills are my long suit."

6. *Interviewer:* "So managing advanced technical scientist types will not be a problem for you?"

   Candidate: "Oh no, not at all. I'm very experienced at managing all types of employees."

7. *Interviewer:* "Are you a real go-getter salesperson, or do you prefer to wait for the customers to come to you?"

   Candidate: "I'm a real go-getter."

8. *Interviewer:* "This position requires a person who can manage multiple priorities for a staff of fifteen individuals. Do you think you could do that?"

   Candidate: "Yes!"

9. *Interviewer:* "Would you rather have a boss who let you operate pretty much on your own or would you prefer a micro-manager?"

   Candidate: "I definitely prefer a boss who trusts me to work on my own."

10. *Interviewer:* "So if you were required to work overtime every now and then, you wouldn't mind?"

    Candidate: "Oh, no. Overtime is a part of every job."

11. *Interviewer:* "This position really needs someone who is flexible because things are always changing around here. Do you consider yourself to be a flexible person—someone who can adapt to change quickly?"

    Candidate: "I'm the most flexible person I know."

12. *Interviewer:* "What we really need is someone who can come in here and hit the ground running."

    Candidate: "Then I'm your man!"

Exercise 8
RESPONDING TO EVASION STRATEGIES

Directions: In the examples below, the candidate is attempting to stall or manipulate his or her way out of answering the question. In the space provided, please design a response such that the candidate is forced to answer the question originally asked. *Suggested Time:* 10 minutes. The answers are provided on pages A-17–A-18 of this workbook.

1. *Interviewer:* "Suppose management put you in charge of a team about whose work you were unfamiliar. What steps would you take to get up to speed as quickly as possible?"

   Candidate: "That sort of thing doesn't actually happen around here, does it?"

2. *Interviewer:* "What specific experience have you had working from a UNIX platform?"

   Candidate: "Well, I do have familiarity with all kinds of platforms."

3. *Interviewer:* "What techniques have you used to coach an employee who is having difficulties, as opposed to coaching a superstar to a higher level of performance?"

   Candidate: "Sometimes it's really satisfying to help someone who would fail without your assistance, and at other times it's rewarding to be a part of an outstanding performer's advancement."

4. *Interviewer:* "Tell me about any difficulties you've encountered as a team leader."

   Candidate: "Are you talking about technical problems, resource problems, design problems, or interpersonal problems?"

5. *Interviewer:* "Please compare the different selling strategies you have used in selling into an established territory of longstanding customers, as opposed to opening up a new territory of customers unfamiliar with your product line."

   Candidate: "Actually I've done both so neither would be a problem."

6. *Interviewer:* "This job requires that you take some advanced technical courses in the evenings. What problems might this create for you?"

   Candidate: "Is everyone in the department required to take these courses?"

7. *Interviewer:* "How would you describe your management style?"

   Candidate: "I'm not exactly sure I understand what you mean."

8. *Interviewer:* "Under what specific circumstances have you involved your staff in your decision making?"

   Candidate: "It really depends on the particular problem involved. Sometimes it's worthwhile to get the staff's input and at other times it's just better to keep your own counsel."

9. *Interviewer:* "What would you do if you discovered that several members of your staff were trading stock on the Internet when they were supposed to be working?"

   Candidate: "I assume this organization has some rules and regulations regarding this sort of thing."

10. *Interviewer:* "If I were to ask your previous boss about your ability to manage others, what do you think she would say?"

    Candidate: "She's actually left the labor market and has gone to live in Europe."

11. *Interviewer:* "What has been your basic strategy for handling a large project that is to be accomplished within an inadequate time frame?"

    Candidate: "Well, it's all a matter of time management, isn't it? If one is organized, such situations are not a problem."

12. *Interviewer:* "What have you done recently to prepare yourself for a job of this type?"

    Candidate: "I'm not sure what you mean."

ADVANCED INTERVIEWING STRATEGIES
(Two-Day Format Only)

Discussion Notes

Resume Analysis

Record Keeping and Related Paperwork
Note Taking

Right of Disclosure

Disclaimer Paragraph

Offer of Employment Letter

Non-Compete Agreements and Employment Contracts

Rapid Screening Technique

1. Construct an MMM® with four or five requirements

2. Inform HR that you only want to see candidates possessing at least four of the five requirements

Round Robin and Team Interviews

Interviewing by Telephone

Hiring Professionals

Professionals are defined as those persons having specialized educational backgrounds and/or degrees (such as engineering or accounting) or those with substantial, extensive experience in a particular field. Their backgrounds qualify them for greater levels of salaried compensation.

Others are defined as those persons whose career backgrounds are much more common in the marketplace (such as clerical personnel, trainees of various kinds, and general administrators). Their backgrounds are less specialized and focused, perhaps because these candidates have not yet set themselves on a firm career path. These persons may be paid on an hourly basis.

The differences between these two groups of candidates will become clear to you in the way each responds to your questioning. Here are the differences you should expect to uncover.

Professionals	Others
require autonomy to do their best work	are more comfortable with some structure
commitment is to their profession	commitment is more likely to their boss/co-workers
identify with their professional peers	identify with their co-workers
standards set by their profession	standards set by their employer/boss
interested in narrow specialization	interested in the organization's issues
money less important than freedom	money more important than freedom
greatest fear: technical obsolescence	greatest fear: being laid off
accept authority on basis of expertise	accept authority on basis of hierarchy
must have challenging work to remain	challenge is nice but not obligatory
key personal factors: judgment, ingenuity, taking initiative, creativity	key personal factors: malleability, adaptability, conformity
work involves one-of-a-kind activities	work involves a variety of activities

Professionals	Others
person shapes the work and its output	the work processes determine the output
few clear objective measures of success	many objective measure of success
typical channels of recruitment don't work	typical channels of recruitment work well
work requires imagination and sagacity	work requires following directions
tasks are based on redesigning (or creating a new) system	tasks are based on maintaining some system or procedure
long-term employment is desirable	short-term employment is normal
person must already have expertise	on-the-job training needed and sufficient
productivity is measured against risk vs. rewards	productivity is measured against objective standards
completion of tasks may be infinite	completion of tasks is usually finite

Hiring "professionals" is one of management's most important decisions because the person will shape the job—not the other way around.

What to look for in a "professional" candidate

Issues that have NO bearing on later job success of a professional

Issues that have GREAT bearing on later job success

Retaining good professionals

PREPARATION
FOR ROLE PLAY

ROLE-PLAY INSTRUCTIONS

Directions: The vacancy for which you are going to interview is the position you most often interview to fill. First, prepare a Master Match Matrix® that covers what a candidate must have, know, or be able to do in order to meet your performance expectations successfully. Then select the ten questions you intend to use when you interview and write them below. Each one of the selected questions MUST assist you in assessing whether or not the candidate meets the criteria in the matrix.

The questions I will use are:

1.

2.

3.

4.

5.

6.

7.

8.

9.

10.

MASTER MATCH MATRIX®

POSITION: _____

Candidate's Name:	first priority competency	second priority competency	third priority competency	fourth priority competency	fifth priority competency	sixth priority competency	seventh priority competency	eighth priority competency	Total score:

Needs ⟶   ⟶ Wants

LEGAL RESTRICTIONS
AND RELATED ISSUES

Legally Restricted Topics

age; date of birth

availability for Saturday and Sunday work

citizenship

color of hair or eyes; height; weight

friends or relatives working for organization

maiden name

Mr., Mrs., Miss

gender

spouse's work; spouse's name

marital status; widowed, divorced, separated

prior married name

children under eighteen; number of children

arrangements for day care of children

arrests

credit record

garnishment record

fidelity bond ever refused

previous Workers' Compensation cases

handicapped

lowest salary candidate will accept

Questions One Cannot Ask During an Interview

1. How old are you? When were you born? What is your date of birth? You seem awfully young to have had so much experience in the industry.

2. What church do you go to? Do you attend religious services regularly? Do you ever have to miss work because of your religion? Do you consider yourself a religious person? Does your religion prevent you from working on weekends (or eating certain foods or drinking with the customers, etc.)? I see you are wearing a cross (or a Star of David); are you Catholic (or Jewish)?

3. What country are you from? You have an interesting accent; where are your people from? I have a friend with a name like yours and he's Armenian (or Polish or Italian); is that what you are?

4. What kind of work does your spouse do? Does your spouse work? How much money does your spouse make? Does your spouse contribute to the family income?

5. How is your family life? Are you married (or divorced, separated, living with anyone, engaged, etc.)? How are you and your spouse getting along? Are you planning to get married (or divorced or separated) in the near future? Why aren't you married?

6. Have you ever been arrested? Have you ever had any trouble with the law? Has a bonding company ever refused to bond you?

7. How's your health? Have you ever collected Workers' Compensation for a job-related injury? Do you have high blood pressure? Are you overweight? Do you have a handicap that would prevent you from meeting the demands of this job? Are you on any type of medication?

8. What is the lowest salary you will accept? What is your minimum salary requirement? How much money do you need? How's your credit rating? How much in debt are you? How much money do you owe?

9. Do you own your own home (or car or other real estate)?

10. How many children to you have? Do you have any children? Why don't you have any children? Are you planning to have children? What are your plans for raising a family?

11. Who will take care of the children while you are at work? How old is your youngest child? If both of you are working, who takes care of the children when they get sick? Will you ever have to miss work because of your children?

12. How do you get along with men (or women)? Most of our customers/clients are male (or female); will you have any problems interfacing with them? How well do you get along with other women (or men)?

13. Your supervisor will be a female (or black or younger than you or older than you); does that create any difficulties for you? How do you feel about working with people of a different race (or of another gender or with younger people or with older people)?

14. You're not a women's libber, are you? What do you think about this Ms. versus Miss or Mrs. business? How do you feel about the "Women's Movement"? Are you a member of NOW? Have you ever filed a sex discrimination case with the EEOC?

15. Do you have to miss work at certain times of the month? What type of birth control do you practice? What are you doing to ensure that you will not get pregnant? Are you doing anything to ensure that child bearing will not interrupt your career plans?

16. Will your spouse mind if you have to be away for long periods on business trips? Does your spouse object to overtime? Will overtime requirements create problems for you at home?

17. Are "you people" good at working with numbers? What are your feelings about black militancy? Did you ever receive public assistance? You will be the only black (or female or foreigner or person over 50 or person under 25) on our sales force (or in this facility); do you think you can handle that OK?

18. What do your parents do? Do you have any brothers or sisters? How many brothers and/or sisters do you have?

19. This is a hectic job—lots of pressure; do you think you can keep up with the younger people on the staff? How do you think you'll fit in with the younger (or older or female or black) members of the staff?

Checking and Giving References

Reference Checking

Reference Giving

Employer Liability

Exercise 9
LEGALITY ISSUES

Directions: In the following exercise, please determine (a) what the problem is and (b) how you think it should be dealt with. *Suggested Time:* 15 minutes. Answers are provided on pages A-18–A-19 of this workbook.

1. The candidate tells you that she has difficulties working with "certain" minorities and asks if you have any of "those" people in your department.

    What is the problem here?

    What should you do?

2. The candidate is interviewing for a job in your warehouse. He tells you that he has spent the last five years in prison for child molestation.

    What is the problem here?

    What should you do?

3. The candidate is extremely well-qualified for the vacancy. However, her physical appearance tells you she is a health risk. She is about 5'5" tall and well over 300 pounds, her face is flushed, and her breathing is labored.

    What is the problem here?

    What should you do?

4. The candidate is dark-skinned with dark hair and eyes. His name is Mudisser Haddar. He claims to be "a red-blooded American from Hawaii." You suspect he is an illegal alien.

    What is the problem here?

    What should you do?

5. You are working with an employment agency to fill a vacancy. You want a young person with the very latest computer skills and advanced technological knowledge. How should you describe your preferences to the agency?

    What is the problem here?

    What should you do?

6. The candidate speaks English very poorly, although her understanding of the language seems adequate. Your job description does not specify fluency in English as a requirement.

    What is the problem here?

    What should you do?

7. The candidate tells you that his references, although excellent, will disclose that he is accident-prone. He has had at least one Workers' Compensation claim at each of his last four jobs.

What is the problem here?

What should you do?

8. The candidate tells you she is in the United States on a temporary visa.

What is the problem here?

What should you do?

9. The candidate comes from another department within your organization. The candidate's current manager tells you that the candidate spends more time on breaks smoking than at her desk working.

What is the problem here?

What should you do?

10. The candidate uses a wheelchair but claims to be physically able to handle the demands of the position (auditor).

What is the problem here?

What should you do?

11. The candidate tells you she has just completed an eight-week secretarial computer course courtesy of the state's "Get-Off-of-Welfare" program. If you hire her, this will be her first job. She proudly tells you that she is a single mom with five little ones at home.

What is the problem here?

What should you do?

12. The candidate is responding to your newspaper advertisement for a telephone customer service representative. His hair is spiked and dyed bright orange; he has rings in his nose, ears, eyebrow, and lower lip. His tee-shirt carries the legend "Life Sucks."

What is the problem here?

What should you do?

13. The candidate is extremely well-qualified for your vacancy of "outside salesperson." He has refused to sign your non-compete agreement, which is a requirement for employment.

    What is the problem here?

    What should you do?

14. The candidate has indicated on her application and also informed you verbally that her son is already employed by the organization in another area.

    What is the problem here?

    What should you do?

15. From the candidate's lengthy experience and general physical appearance, you judge him to be in his early sixties.

    What is the problem here?

    What should you do?

16. The vacancy requires "availability for Saturday and Sunday work." The candidate tells you that Saturdays are religious days for him.

    What is the problem here?

    What should you do?

17. The candidate claims that the references from her last employer will probably be very negative because she filed a sexual harassment case against her boss, which has still to be adjudicated in the courts.

    What is the problem here?

    What should you do?

18. On his resume, the candidate has listed membership in the following organizations: Alcoholics Anonymous, The Fraternal Order of Christians Against Euthanasia, and the Italian-American Brotherhood for a Democratic Majority.

    What is the problem here?

    What should you do?

19. According to the candidate's paperwork, she has spent the last two years in a facility for the mentally ill.

    What is the problem here?

    What should you do?

20. In answer to the question, "For what reason did you decide to leave your last position," the candidate replies, "The Feds put a garnishment on my wages for back taxes. I thought declaring bankruptcy got rid of all your debts but I guess I was wrong."

    What is the problem here?

    What should you do?

21. The candidate is extremely well-qualified for the position. She asks that your organization NOT check references at her present job because she is likely to be immediately terminated if her boss discovers that she is out looking for another job.

    What is the problem here?

    What should you do?

22. You verbally offered the candidate a position with a salary of $60,000 per year and she verbally accepted. The human resources department then sent her an "offer letter" stating the salary as $5,000 per month. The candidate is upset and asks that the letter be revised to reflect the $60,000 per year you originally quoted her.

    What is the problem here?

    What should you do?

23. In answer to the question on the company application, "Have you been convicted of a felony within the last five years?" the candidate has responded "yes" but provided no explanation.

    What is the problem here?

    What should you do?

24. The candidate is very pregnant and asks if your organization discriminates against women in her condition.

    What is the problem here?

    What should you do?

ROLE-PLAY GUIDELINES

Instructions

If You Are an Observer
- Listen
- Take Notes
- Give Feedback

If You Are Playing the Interviewer
- Be Yourself
- Use Matrix and Questions You Have Prepared
- See Candidate's Resume

If You Are Playing the Candidate
- Use Role Cards
- Use Your History
- Have Fun

Time Frame
- Each interview will be 5 minutes long
- Then there will be 3 minutes for feedback

Questioning Strategy for Role-Play Activities

When You Are Playing a Candidate

- Respond to all closed-ended questions with either "YES" or "NO"

When You Are Playing the Interviewer

- Begin every question with "WHAT," "WHEN," "WHERE," "WHO," "HOW," or "WHY" (use "why" sparingly)

When You Are an Observer

- Jump in immediately should you hear a "Barbara Walters" question; ask the role player to re-work the question

- Notice and comment on how the interviewer began the exchange

- Notice and comment on any candidate responses that were not appropriately followed up on

- Notice and comment on how (and if) the interviewer maintained the observer-catalyst position

PEOPLE READING
AND PERSONALITY FIT

Discussion Notes

Analyzing the Work Environment

Leadership Style of Manager

Nature of Work Team

Tasks Involved

Background of "People Reading"

Three Motivational Types

1. The task-oriented candidate
   Common word patterns

   Body language

   Interviewing behaviors

   Strengths

   Possible problems after hiring

2. The affiliation-oriented candidate
   Common word patterns

   Body language

   Interviewing behaviors

   Strengths

   Possible problems after hiring

3. The power-oriented candidate
   Common word patterns

   Body language

   Interviewing behaviors

   Strengths

   Possible problems after hiring

Note Taking on People Reading

To incorporate *people reading* into your note taking, write T (task), A (affiliation), and P (power) across the top of your note paper. Each time a candidate says something that indicates a bias toward one of these types, make a mark in that column. At the end of the interview, you will likely have some marks in all three columns, but one column will likely have many more marks than the other two, indicating this candidate's motivational predisposition.

Candidate Presentation During the Interview

	Task/Achievement	Affiliation	Power
Words Used	efficient, effective; difficult, challenging; quality, excellence; new, different; dependability, responsibility	nice, cooperation, team effort; needed and helping, happy family; not making waves	uses titles, drops names; wants "more important" work image; caliber; job was beneath me
Body Language	stiff and formal; may fidget; maintains physical distance	nods head "yes"; smiles a lot; maintains close proximity	sits relaxed; spreads out; uses expansive hand gestures
Dress	preference for dark colors	preference for bright colors and patterns	dresses well; well-groomed; may wear initials; may wear or carry status items
Other Behaviors	wants everything in writing; may bring lots of documentation	tells you what he thinks you want to hear; "anxious to please"	asks about org chart, reporting relationships, and promotional opportunities
Demeanor	very serious; minimum of friendly chit-chat; businesslike	relaxed and informal; warm and friendly	manipulative; "salesman" type; slick
References Say	workaholic, compulsive; human relations problems, things are either right or wrong; hard worker	dislikes change; has difficulty making decisions; hard to get a straight answer from; cooperative and pleasant; not a hard worker	works around the rules; quite an ego; likes to impress others; always looking for a deal; too concerned about his/her reputation
Strengths	hard worker; dedicated to excellence and perfection; good problem solver	strong human relations; works without structure	natural leader; good, strong political skills; flexible

Possible Behavior Issues After Hiring

Dimensions of the Work Situation	Affiliation	Power	Task
delegation	haphazard	well-planned	reluctant; partial
concern for quality	reasonable is fine	wants excellence	demands perfection
giving feedback	mostly praises	tells good and bad	mostly critical
temperament	nice guy	even-tempered	moody; angry
about mistakes	accepts as normal	What can we learn?	Whose fault is it?
handling problems	ignores	tries to prevent	likes to solve
organizational skills	disorganized	reasonably organized	precise and exact
making requests	hints	asks and suggests	directs and orders
making decisions	lets fall to others	consults with staff	by themselves
sensitive issues	sympathetic and inquisitive	political and tactful	blunt and tactless
main job interest	acceptance and inclusion	leadership and power	excellence and challenge
self-perception	friend	leader	expert
regard for rules	goes along with	uses and bends	enforces to the letter
biggest problem	decision making	not enough authority	other people
a challenge is	handling change	taking charge	difficult task
human relations	warm and friendly	congenial and objective	cool and distant
work preference	work with others	leadership role	work alone
responsibility	too much already	pushes for more	guards his or her own
staff's ideas	excited but no support	may take credit for	only own are good
handling conflict	runs away	negotiates	confronts

Exercise 10
PEOPLE READING

Directions: Please identify the following candidate types from their speech patterns and speculate on the types of behavior problems each MIGHT bring into the workplace. *Suggested Time:* 10 minutes. The answers are provided on pages A-23–A24 of this workbook.

1. "I like a difficult and challenging job, and I'm not afraid of a little hard work either."

   This candidate is:

   Some behavior issues might be:

2. "The most aggravating thing about that job was that I couldn't hire and fire my own staff. There was also a lot of unnecessary red tape to keep you from doing anything unique."

   This candidate is:

   Some behavior issues might be:

3. "I worked very closely with the director of marketing and even played golf periodically with the corporate vice president."

   This candidate is:

   Some behavior issues might be:

4. "Most of all, I liked the people I worked with. Everyone was very nice. We all got along really well."

   This candidate is:

   Some behavior issues might be:

5. "What I'm really looking for in a job is meaningful work and a boss who will demand and appreciate quality results, achievement, and creativity."

   This candidate is:

   Some behavior issues might be:

6. "When the new company took us over, everything changed. It wasn't a comfortable place to work any more. Also, a lot of my friends were laid off."

This candidate is:

Some behavior issues might be:

7. "It is important to me that my job title help promote the image of competency, authority, and visibility necessary for me to do this job."

This candidate is:

Some behavior issues might be:

8. "I want to be evaluated according to my contribution. I'm tired of working with organizations that reward longevity instead of competence."

This candidate is:

Some behavior issues might be:

9. I have friends who work here and they said this was a nice place."

This candidate is:

Some behavior issues might be:

10. "Do you have casual Fridays here?"

This candidate is:

Some behavior issues might be:

11. "If I decide to continue my education by taking courses in night school, what kinds of promotional opportunities can I expect?"

This candidate is:

Some behavior issues might be:

12. "Delegation has always been a problem because invariably others will not meet my expectations for a quality result."

This candidate is:

Some behavior issues might be:

Exercise 11
WRAP-UP

Directions: Please complete the following statements in the spaces provided. *Suggested Time:* 5 minutes. Answers are provided on pages A-24–A-25 of this workbook.

1. The most important skill in interviewing is _____.

2. The interviewer should speak only _____ percent of the time.

3. The candidate's success on the job will be determined by my _____.

4. The best time to prepare for the interview is _____.

5. The only way to encourage a reticent candidate to speak is to _____.

6. The best interview questions offer no hint as to _____.

7. Most interviewing errors are caused by the use of too many _____ questions.

8. A good match (candidate-to-job) requires that the interviewer uncover _____.

9. The problem with using direct questions is _____.

10. The problem with using the laundry-list question is _____.

11. The candidate's body language cues are a key to _____.

12. Starting the interview with a structuring statement will help me _____.

13. If the candidate answers in generalities, I should ask a _____.

14. If the response does not relate to the question asked, I should _____.

15. Truly effective interviewing requires separating _____ from _____.

16. Starting an interview by talking about hobbies and such is _____.

17. Asking candidates about their weaknesses is _____.

18. When a candidate tries to avoid answering a question, _____.

19. "Dumb" questions are those which (1) _____ (2) _____ (3) _____ and (4) _____.

20. The most important segment of the interview is _____.

Directions: In the space provided, please indicate how the interviewer should respond in order to move the conversation productively forward. *Suggested Time:* 10 minutes. Answers are provided on page A-25 of this workbook.

1. *Candidate:* "I really enjoy supervising and I think I'm pretty good at it too."

   Interviewer:

2. *Candidate:* "My manager just couldn't understand why the project took so much time. It was really a very bad situation for me."

   Interviewer:

3. *Candidate:* "Team leadership is no problem for me. I've had lots of experience doing that."

   Interviewer:

4. *Candidate:* "I may be over 50 but I can still run circles around the 30-year-olds you've got working here."

   Interviewer:

5. *Candidate:* "The company was unclear about its market strategy; my department head was the most disorganized person you could ever meet; and my lazy staff were only there for their pay-checks. So I was forced to spend all my time putting out fires and doing everyone else's jobs."

   Interviewer:

6. *Candidate:* "The job was very interesting but now . . . I guess . . . it's time for me to move on."

   Interviewer:

7. *Candidate:* "What I'm really looking for in a job is more of a challenge."

   Interviewer:

8. *Candidate:* "All my previous bosses thought I was a quick study and a very fast learner."

   Interviewer:

9. *Candidate:* "Don't you think that the person you hire should be a good people person—you know, cooperative and such so that they will fit right in?"

   Interviewer:

10. *Candidate:* "Well, I am familiar with performance management and the concept of the learning organization."

    Interviewer:

11. *Candidate:* "I guess it really depends on the particular project. Sometimes I really enjoy working with a team, and at other times it just seems more practical to work alone."

    Interviewer:

12. *Candidate:* "I really like working with people."

    Interviewer:

APPENDICES

COMMON ERRORS IN CONDUCTING THE INTERVIEW

1. Failing to establish rapport with the candidate

    Rapport is not about "making friends" with the candidate. Neither is it about playing psychologist to the candidate's anxiety. Rapport is accomplished by stating at the onset how the interview will be structured.

2. Not knowing exactly what information is required; not working from a meticulously developed list of requirements

    Job descriptions list duties, activities, and responsibilities; they do not detail expectations or results to be achieved. Without this kind of information, there is no way to analyze or measure a candidate's past performance against the needs of the vacant position.

3. Becoming a victim of the "halo effect"

    This can occur in two ways. The first is when the interviewer finds something in the candidate's background that matches something in his or her own (such as attending the same university or having grown up in the same state). That similarity gives the entire interview a golden glow so that, when negative information surfaces, the tendency is to play it down or ignore it. The second way the "halo" can occur is when the interviewer finds the candidate possesses outstanding abilities in one area and then assumes the person is equally superior in other areas.

4. Doing most of the talking

    Most untrained interviewers talk too much and therefore fail to obtain meaningful information about the candidate. The interviewer should only speak about 20 percent of the time. The most important skill in interviewing is listening. The only time one can listen to a candidate is when he or she is speaking.

5. Not allowing silences to occur

   The only way that interviewers can influence reluctant candidates to speak is by keeping silent themselves (with body language that says, "I'm awaiting your next words"). More often than not, however, the reason for the silence is that the candidate is thinking. When the interviewer fills the silence, he or she has effectively derailed the candidate's train of thought.

6. Using too many direct questions (questions answerable by "yes" or "no")

   This type of question minimizes the amount of information received; it discourages the candidate from speaking freely; and it prevents the interview from flowing smoothly. The most significant issue of all is that direct questions prevent the interviewer from learning how the candidate thinks.

7. Asking questions that serve no purpose

   Without adequate preparation—which includes a pre-selected battery of questions to be asked—the interviewer may ask irrelevant questions just to take up air time while being mentally engaged in conjuring up the next question. Moreover, the candidate recognizes that the interviewer is engaged in question generation rather than in listening.

8. Poor sequencing of questions

   Without designing a structure beforehand, the interviewer will jump around from area to area in the questioning. The result is superficial information from many areas of the candidate's background but no in-depth knowledge of any single area.

9. Making impulsive conclusions and generalizations based on some assumed characteristic

   Interviewers' biases may work against them by influencing them to recommend hiring the candidate based on appearance ("looks the part"), verbal facility ("thinks well on his feet"), and apparent values ("honest and forthright; she looked me straight in the eye").

10. Repeating the information on the application or resume

    This wastes everyone's time, but it is an excellent ploy for someone who is not prepared to conduct an interview. Unfortunately, such an approach signals the candidate that the organization has no interest in him or her.

11. Selling the organization too soon

Telling the candidate all the things that the interviewer believes make the position challenging, rewarding, advantageous, and exciting will not make it attractive to the candidate, no matter how enthusiastically the interviewer imparts the information. The only way to find out what excites candidates about a job—any job—is to allow them to tell their own stories.

12. Ignoring intuition (the old "gut feelings")

Intuitive feelings are the result of facts, observation (of the candidate's body language), and experience coming together on a subconscious level. It is vital to substantiate intuitive messages with more incisive data. A cardinal rule in interviewing is, "When in doubt, don't hire." Intuition is a signal to the interviewer when more definitive information is needed.

13. Asking questions that don't give worthwhile information

Included in this category are (1) questions that telegraph the desired responses ("This job requires exceptionally good listening skills. Are you a good listener?"); (2) apparent choices where there are none ("Do you get emotional and overreact or can you keep a cool head?"); and (3) questions where the answers, although obvious, cannot be checked for truthfulness ("Do you have good common sense?").

14. Asking "magic" questions

Questions of this nature are supposed to provide penetrating information about the candidate's personality ("If you could be an animal, which one would you choose?" "What do you think is the meaning of life?"). Such questions are an excuse for not doing the real investigative work required for an effective interview.

15. Not being knowledgeable about the legal restrictions regarding interviewing

There are two problems here. Should the interviewer ask an illegal question, the company could face an expensive lawsuit. On the other hand, if the interviewer is unclear about what can and cannot be asked, he or she may fail to do a thorough interview, fearing that a topic might be illegal.

16. Giving evaluative feedback; exchanging opinions with the candidate

It is not the function of the interviewer to "hold up his or her end of the conversation" by commenting on or evaluating what the candidate has said. The interview is not a social event; the interviewer's opinions are not a concern here.

17. Asking multiple choice (laundry-list) questions

Questions that contain too many issues elicit only partial responses. In addition, they allow the candidate to escape the task of thinking by simply selecting a response from the list of choices provided by the interviewer.

18. Excessive note taking

Voluminous notes make it impossible to cull out the important data afterward. Moreover, when an interviewer's attention is consumed with note taking, there is little eye contact and therefore scant opportunity to relate to the candidate. At the end of the dialogue, the interviewer may have no sense of the character or personality of the candidate.

19. Giving commitments; making promises

Even innocent comments such as, "We always provide our superior performers with significant financial rewards" can be interpreted as an inducement to join the organization or as a commitment for a job.

20. Using the candidate's resume as the foundation of the interview

Starting the interview process by asking the candidate to clarify various issues on the resume (the usual strategy) means that every interview will be examining different items. Because every resume is different, each candidate's evaluation is based on a moving target rather than on anything grounded and solid. Therefore, any evaluation process cannot possibly be objective.

ANSWERS
TO THE EXERCISES

Interviewing Quiz

1. True   Unless interviewers prepare some kind of yardstick against which to judge the appropriateness of each candidate, they will be victimized by their mood, their prejudices, and other non-essential issues such as the candidate's physical appearance.

2. False It is almost impossible to be objective no matter how skilled an interviewer may be.

3. True   Such qualities ensure a comfortable, pleasant exchange. It is easy to think positively and overlook the shortcomings of a person who is easy to be with, even though those qualities may have nothing to do with the job.

4. False In the interview, the candidate is putting his or her best foot forward; after the person is employed, the other foot becomes visible. There is often a vast difference.

5. False Those hired today will shape the future of the company. Therefore, poor quality hiring today may result in poor leadership decisions, disastrous market strategy, dreadful customer service, and other problems tomorrow. Faulty hiring also causes excessive and costly turnover.

6. True   Candidates are much more likely to be judged on how well they get along with the interviewer than on how well they meet the requirements for the job.

7. True   People tend to be more comfortable with those who are most like them; folks who think the same way, have similar beliefs, come from the same part of the country, and so on.

In romantic situations, opposites attract, but in business, similarities are more likely to attract. This can even include physical appearance.

8. False   The most appealing candidates are those already employed. Unemployed candidates raise concerns about why they are currently without a job. Moreover, they often seem anxious and distressed.

9. False   Candidates with non-traditional backgrounds and unconventional ideas are most likely to be disqualified; such candidates are considered risky.

10. False   Stress interviews were developed for selecting spies. The strategy is to attack the candidate personally and psychologically. Using stress interviews for employment is inappropriate; job stress is task-related.

11. True   The purpose of the interview is to learn about the candidate. This cannot happen if the interviewer is doing most of the talking.

12. False   The candidate may be nervous and the conversation erratic. The interviewer, however, is only responsible for learning enough about the candidate to judge his or her appropriateness for the job.

13. False   Additional information may be necessary such as college transcript, proof of state license, bonding clearance, medical information, references, etc.

14. False   The human mind cannot effectively listen and evaluate simultaneously. Since the only opportunity for listening occurs when the candidate is there, it seems wise to concentrate on listening then and to save the evaluation process for later, after the candidate leaves.

15. False   Competent interviewers respect their gut feelings. They will, however, follow up on any intuitive notions by seeking additional corroborating data.

16. False   It is best to evaluate the candidate as soon as he or she leaves the interview, while the interaction can be easily recalled. A delay may make it difficult to remember exactly what was said.

17. True The interviewer acts as an agent for the company. As such, the company is liable for any illegal actions made by its agent.

18. False Not all jobs require someone in them who is promotable.

19. True Data gathering requires listening; evaluation requires thinking. The human mind cannot do both simultaneously and do them well. When the evaluation process goes on during data gathering, important information may be lost because the interviewer was evaluating while the candidate was talking.

20. False Asking such questions in the interview is illegal. The candidate could easily sue the company and win.

21. True Smart candidates will analyze an interviewer's question, listening for a clue as to the "right" answer—the answer the interviewer wants to hear.

22. True There are many studies that indicate such determinations are made in under 5 seconds; the remainder of the interview focuses on confirming that initial impression.

23. True Learning about the candidate can only be accomplished by listening while the candidate speaks.

24. False Serious legal problems can result when a candidate volunteers personal information. The candidate could sue alleging that this personal information was provided in response to the interviewer's question. It is impossible to defend against such an allegation.

25. True The interview doesn't measure anything. It only provides the skilled interviewer with some very strong indications regarding competence, commitment, and human relations.

Exercise 1

1. How would you go about coaching an employee about his or her lack of attention to detail?

2. How would you ensure that your staff members freely share information with one another?

3. Tell me about a time when your manager asked you for feedback on a peer's performance.

4. Suppose changes were imminent. How far in advance would you inform your staff?

5. How have you coached an employee who had problems identifying his or her priorities?

6. How would you go about playing the role of mediator in a conflict situation?

7. Tell me about a situation when your manager wanted to terminate an employee and you thought the person might be saved with some solid coaching efforts. How was that situation resolved?

8. What strategies have you used to ensure your own objectivity when giving performance feedback to an annoying staff member?

9. Suppose you were told to step outside the boundaries of your experience and knowledge to solve a serious problem. How would you start the solution process?

10. Tell me about an instance when you saw or experienced an unethical situation at work.

11. Describe for me the critical qualities in the best manager you ever had.

12. How would you go about coaching risk taking in others?

Exercise 2

1. (a) What strategies have you used in order to build and maintain an atmosphere of trust in your department?

    (b) How have you determined the developmental needs of each employee who reports to you?

    (c) How often and under what circumstances do you involve your staff in your decision-making and problem-solving efforts?

2. (a) How would you describe what has been your basic business philosophy?

    (b) What evidence can you point to that illustrates your personal values and beliefs as they operate on the job?

    (c) In your attempts to structure the ideal work environment, what kinds of staff behaviors do you encourage and reward? What behaviors do you try to discourage?

3. (a) What has been the most insightful piece of learning you have gained from participating in a team effort? How have you used that learning in succeeding situations?

   (b) In your previous work experience as a peer professional member of a team, how were leadership issues typically resolved?

   (c) What has been your experience with conflict resolution in a team setting where outside intervention was not utilized?

4. (a) Some people are said to roll with the punches. Describe a situation in which you demonstrated this sort of skill.

   (b) Please describe a situation that demonstrates your flexibility.

   (c) Tell me about a situation where more responsibility was thrust on you unexpectedly.

5. (a) I'd like to hear about the most challenging communication situation you have ever come up against. What made it challenging? How did you handle it?

   (b) Describe an occasion when you were interacting with someone who was not communicating clearly. How were you able to respond effectively?

   (c) What strategies have you used to "sell" your ideas to your boss and/or higher management?

6. (a) Tell me about a time when you went above and beyond the call of duty. What motivated you to make that extra effort?

   (b) Relate an incident where you secured resources that were difficult to obtain but which were necessary in order for you to achieve a goal.

   (c) Describe a time when you responded to rejection by trying an alternative approach.

7. (a) Tell me about a situation when you were presented with a project that had no history, guidelines, or structure other than a due date. How did you start?

   (b) In your last position, what problems did you identify that had been previously overlooked? What, if anything, did you do about them?

   (c) Tell me about some of the changes that occurred in your last job because of you.

8. (a) Tell me about a time when you had to influence someone higher up in the organization who had a reputation for being hard-headed.

   (b) In previous jobs, what type of person have you found is most difficult to work with? What did you do in order to work productively with such a person?

   (c) Tell me about a situation when your boss was upset about a decision you had made. How did you handle your boss's anger?

9. (a) Describe a situation in which you had to be analytical and thorough in making a critical decision. Walk me through the process you followed.

   (b) Tell me about a time in your life when you had mixed feelings about what to do. How did you sort things out so that you could arrive at some closure?

   (c) On previous jobs, what was the basis on which you determined whether to take on tasks, projects, or responsibilities that were not assigned to you or even expected of you?

10. (a) In your previous job, what techniques did you use to develop and maintain existing customers?

    (b) Tell me about the toughest sale you ever made. Describe how you convinced your client to buy.

    (c) Describe how you influenced a customer to purchase your higher priced product when he or she had been buying a similar, lower priced product from a competitor.

11. (a) Please describe a situation in which you were able to turn a negative customer around. What was the issue? How did you accomplish the turnaround?

    (b) Describe a situation when the customer's perception of what occurred was clearly wrong. How did you go about resolving the problem?

    (c) Tell me about a time when you were dealing with a customer who wanted his or her problem resolved in a way that was detrimental to the company. What did you do?

12. (a) Describe a situation when your skills in diplomacy and patience were put to the test.

     (b)   Give me an example of significant and unrealistic pressure from senior management and how you dealt with that.

     (c)   In what areas do you typically have the least amount of patience at work when it comes to staff problems? What do you do when such situations occur?

Exercise 3

1. Behavioral question
2. Direct question
3. Clarifying question
4. Puzzle question
5. Puzzle question
6. Behavioral question
7. Puzzle question
8. Direct question
9. Puzzle question
10. Clarifying question
11. Encouragement
12. Behavioral question

Exercise 4

1. When the candidate tries to avoid answering the question
2. To uncover how the candidate thinks and makes decisions
3. To start the interview so as to maintain control
4. To discover how the candidate reacts and behaves in real-life situations
5. To encourage the candidate to evaluate him- or herself; to uncover what the candidate thinks of him- or herself (self-image)
6. To encourage the candidate to keep talking along the same lines
7. To assure the candidate that what he or she just said will not harm his or her candidacy and to move the conversation along quickly

8. To force the candidate to be more specific

9. To encourage the candidate to provide lots of information

10. This is not a useful tool and should never be used as a strategy

11. To go after very specific quantitative information

12. To respond to what the interviewer sees reflected in the candidate's body language

Exercise 5

1. *Negative:* The candidate believes we should offer signing bonuses.

   "My sense is this was not the answer you expected."

2. *Negative:* The candidate's response is a lie.

   "Tell me about some of the experiences you've had making such decisions."

3. *Negative:* The candidate is very upset about this line of questioning.

   "I gather things did not go well for you."

4. *Positive:* The candidate is excited by this line of questioning.

   "What enabled you to achieve such remarkable results?"

5. *Negative:* The candidate really dislikes working with teens.

   "Tell me about some specific encounters you've had with teens as customers."

6. *Confusion:* Candidate knows nothing about this topic; response is an attempt to avoid saying anything substantive.

   "Please give me a specific example of how you negotiated for such things as the division of scarce resources between a number of departments, priorities between peers who report to different areas, and so on."

7. *Negative:* The candidate does not want to work with customers.

   "I sense that customer contact is something you'd like to avoid."

8. *Positive:* If presented with the opportunity, the candidate may opt for doing sports over the responsibilities of the job.

   "How have you managed the demands of your job versus the demands of soccer at previous jobs?"

9. *Negative:* The candidate definitely does not want to pursue this line of questioning.

   "I take it there's more to it than that."

10. *Very negative:* Candidate's references will probably not be good.

    "I sense there may be something else we need to cover before we go any further. Because if your references do not work out, you would be terminated immediately."

11. *Negative:* The candidate knows nothing about the topic under discussion and is attempting to avoid answering with anything substantial.

    "Think of a specific situation and tell me how your initiative helped you."

12. *Positive:* The interviewer "hit the nail on the head."

    "What specific efforts did you make to get clear goals and objectives from your boss?"

Exercise 6

1. *Concerns:* Is this a pattern of blaming others for failures? Does this comment show that the candidate is unable to learn from his or her mistakes?

   Question: "Describe a situation where you learned something critical as a result of a mistake you made."

2. *Concern:* If I have a strict 9 to 5 operation, will this candidate be able to adjust?

   Question: "What experience have you had working in a traditional 9 to 5 operation?"

3. *Concerns:* Is this a person who is careless? Will he or she be lax on follow-through?

   Question: "Tell me about a time when you were responsible for all kinds of nitpicking details on a complicated project. How did you manage those details?"

4. *Concerns:* Will I have to continually remind him or her to submit paperwork? Will I have to require that he or she redo paperwork because it is poorly done?

Question: "How have you handled your paperwork at previous jobs?"

5. *Concerns:* Will this candidate cheat on his or her expense account here? What is his or her level of integrity?

   Question: "How did you and your boss happen to decide that padding your expense account was an appropriate way to level the playing field?"

6. *Concerns:* Will this candidate's references be negative? Is this person likely to involve him- or herself in unnecessary, self-generated paperwork?

   Question: "In previous jobs, how have you balanced the need to complete projects on time with your desire to ensure a high level of quality by utilizing these self-imposed quality procedures?"

7. *Concern:* Does this candidate have a problem with human relations? Can this person work effectively in a team setting?

   Question: "Tell me about your experience working with others on a team."

8. *Concerns:* Does this candidate have problems working with women? Does this candidate have problems interacting with others whom he or she consider to be below him- or herself in terms of education or professionalism?

   Question: "What strategies have you used in previous jobs for interacting with non-professionals and the support staff?"

9. *Concern:* Will this person be taking full advantage of every legitimate reason the company allows for an employee to miss work?

   Question: "For what reasons did you have to miss work over the past twelve months?"

10. *Concern:* Will this candidate concentrate more on social and other non-work activities than on his or her job?

    Question: "What kinds of work-related tasks and projects give you the most satisfaction?"

11. *Concern:* Is there something about that job that the candidate doesn't want me to know about—something that might make me decide he or she is not right for this job?

    Question: "I would still like to hear what you learned from that job."

12. *Concern:* Does this candidate actually know how to manage others or does he or she use a one-style-fits-all approach?

Question: "How often and under what circumstances have you varied this approach to managing?"

Exercise 7

1. "Please give me an example of a tough decision you had to make quickly."
2. "Tell me about an occasion when this ability was critical to your success."
3. "Give me an example of a situation when being a self-starter was important."
4. "What techniques have you used that enable you to handle stress so successfully?"
5. "Tell me about a situation where this skill was critical to your success."
6. "Give me a specific example from your previous job that illustrates your ability to manage technical specialists."
7. "I'd like to hear about a few specific instances when you utilized a go-getter approach to land some new accounts."
8. "What strategies or methods have you used in such situations?"
9. "What has been your most recent experience working on your own?"
10. "Tell me about the overtime required of you at your last position."
11. "Give me some examples of your flexibility in the work situation."
12. "Tell me about a time when you were able to 'hit the ground running.'"

Exercise 8

1. "It might be, so suppose management put you in charge of a team about whose work you were unfamiliar. What steps would you take to get up to speed as quickly as possible?"
2. "Give me some specific examples of projects you've worked on utilizing a UNIX platform."

3. "What techniques have you used to coach an employee who is having difficulties, as opposed to coaching a superstar to a higher level of performance?"

4. "I'd like to hear about all types of problems you've encountered as a team leader."

5. "Give me an example of each."

6. "Yes. This job requires that you take some advanced technical courses in the evenings. What problems might this create for you?"

7. "What type of management behavior do you use in order to stimulate your staff to achieve organizational goals?"

8. "Give me an example of each circumstance from your most recent job."

9. "We do. However, what I'd like to know is what would you do if you discovered that several members of your staff were trading stock on the Internet when they were supposed to be working?"

10. "If I were to ask your previous boss about your ability to manage others, what do you think she would say?"

11. "I'd like to hear about such a situation and how you handled it."

12. "What steps have you taken to ensure that you have the skills needed for this position well in hand?"

Exercise 9

1. (a) If hired, this candidate might cause some ugly discrimination problems.

   (b) State that the organization is an Equal Opportunity Employer and therefore hires people without regard to race or ethnic origin and that she probably would not be happy here. Remove her from further consideration. (Discriminating against a bigot does not constitute grounds for legal action.)

2. (a) He has served his time, so you should not deny him the position if he is qualified. Deep down, however, you probably do not want him working for you.

   (b) Search for a candidate with better working experience or qualifications (many years working in a warehouse environment) than this candidate.

3. (a) Neither you nor the candidate is qualified to make a determination about her health.

   (b) If you consider her a serious contender for the position, send the candidate for a medical exam. Brief the doctor first on the physical and mental demands of the job and let the doctor make the health determination. Remember, however, you must treat all candidates the same. If you send this candidate for a medical exam, you must also send all other serious contenders for this position for a medical exam as well.

4. (a) It is common practice to take the candidate's word regarding his or her color, race, and national origin.

   (b) Discuss your concerns with human resources and let them handle it.

5. (a) It would be illegal for you to say "young" or "recent graduate" (because that also indicates young), which relates to age discrimination.

   (b) "What I'm looking for is someone with the latest, most advanced technological knowledge in computer hardware/software."

6. (a) Disqualifying this candidate from further consideration on the basis of something not specified in the job description would leave you open to suit for discrimination.

   (b) If this candidate is otherwise qualified, you must consider her application seriously. If you decide to eliminate her from further consideration, it must be on the basis of something other than her poor command of the language (not enough experience, lack of education, etc.).

7. (a) Legally you cannot eliminate this candidate from consideration due to his many Workers' Compensation claims, even though you know hiring him would make your organization's insurance company very unhappy.

   (b) If you consider him a serious contender for the position, send the candidate for a medical exam. Brief the doctor first on the physical and mental demands of the job and let the doctor make the health determination. Remember, however, you must treat all candidates the same. If you send this candidate for a medical exam, you must also send all other serious contenders for this position for a medical exam as well.

8. (a) Often, "temporary visas" restrict the person to educational pursuits only; working is not allowed. If the temporary visa allows the person to work and your vacancy requires someone with a "security clearance," there may also be a problem.

(b) Human resources would be handling any issues of this nature.

9. (a) There is no problem here because (1) you can deny a person employment on the basis of being a smoker, so there is no legal grounds for suit on this issue; and (2) the candidate is already employed by your organization, so there is no basis for suit regarding the bad reference.

(b) Seek another candidate; say "no" to this one.

10. (a) If your department is wheelchair accessible (which by law it should be), there is no problem.

(b) If the candidate is otherwise qualified, hire him. You cannot deny employment to someone because of a handicap.

11. (a) The candidate has just given you information that legally you should not have (her marital status and the number and age of her children). Legally you cannot deny her employment on the basis of this information.

(b) Tell the candidate, "All hiring in this organization is based only on a person's skills and qualifications for the particular position. Anyone hired into the organization understands that he or she must be there every day on time. Will that present a problem for you?" Then, if she asserts that she will be there every day on time, you must consider her application without regard for her family situation.

12. (a) Unless "appearance" is a requirement for the position and so stated in the job description, you must consider this person's application in spite of how he looks. What is troubling, however, is the legend on his tee-shirt. He may not have the appropriate attitude for a customer service position.

(b) Question the candidate heavily regarding his attitude regarding service and helping people.

13. (a) If signing a non-compete agreement is a requirement for employment and he refuses to sign, then you cannot consider him a viable candidate. If you hire him without him signing the agreement, you create a situation that legally nullifies all

the other non-compete agreements signed by your other outside salespeople.

    (b)   Seek another candidate; say "no" to this one.

14. (a)   You cannot legally deny a person employment on the basis that a relative already works in the organization. It is legally advisable to ensure that one does not work for the other or that both are assigned to the same department.

    (b)   If the candidate is otherwise qualified, you must seriously consider her application.

15. (a)   To deny this candidate serious consideration would be to engage in age discrimination, which is legal grounds for a suit.

    (b)   Forget about his probable age; evaluate him on the basis of his skills, knowledge, and general qualifications for the position.

16. (a)   The issue here is religion. Even though you did not ask, he has provided you with information you should not have. If you hire him, you will have to make "reasonable accommodation for his religious needs." (This is the exact wording in the law.)

    (b)   If the job description clearly stated "This job requires availability for Saturday and Sunday work," then the candidate has disqualified himself from further consideration.

17. (a)   You might suspect she is a troublemaker.

    (b)   Legally you cannot discriminate against her on the basis that she has a legal case going against her former employer. If she is otherwise qualified, you must seriously consider her application.

18. (a)   The candidate has furnished you with information you should not have. If you deny him a job, you could be sued on the basis of religious or national origin or political or handicapped discrimination.

    (b)   Tell the candidate, "All hiring in this organization is based only on a person's skills and qualifications for the particular position. It is not based on religion, national origin, political, or other organizational affiliation. Therefore, please resubmit your paperwork with those affiliations left off."

19. (a)   You cannot discriminate against this candidate because of a prior illness.

(b) If you consider her a serious contender for the position (based on her skills, experience, etc.), send the candidate for a medical exam. Brief the doctor first on the physical and mental demands of the job and let the doctor make the health determination. Remember, however, you must treat all candidates the same. If you send this candidate for a medical exam, you must also send all other serious contenders for this position for a medical exam as well.

20. (a) You cannot discriminate against this candidate based on his or her financial situation unless financial impeccability is a requirement for the position (which might be the case for a financial counselor, investment person, stockbroker, etc.) and is so stated in the job description.

(b) Forget about this information and evaluate the candidate based on his or her skills, experience, and other general qualifications for the position.

21. (a) She has asked that you keep her application confidential with regard to her present employer. You cannot violate her request for confidentiality.

(b) Tell the candidate, "Please understand that if you are hired and if you accept the position, we will be checking your references during the first week of your employment. If your references do not work out, you will be terminated at that point."

22. (a) If the candidate's offer letter states "$60,000/year" and she leaves within the first year, the company is legally liable for payment of the entire $60,000. If the offer letter states $5,000/month and she leaves within the first year, the company is liable for only one month's salary.

(b) Ask human resources to redo the offer letter stating $60,000/year pro-rated.

23. (a) You'd like to know if the crime might somehow impact the job but you are unsure how to approach the problem.

(b) The candidate has obviously served his or her time so you cannot deny him or her serious consideration (skills, experience, qualifications, etc.) for the position. Make sure, however, that you alert human resources to the issue and let them investigate it before you make a job offer.

24. (a) The problem is you cannot discriminate against her because of her condition, even though you know as soon as she gets on board she will be taking a pregnancy leave.

(b) Tell the candidate, "All hiring in this organization is based only on a person's skills and qualifications for the particular position and not on physical condition" (unless that is a requirement for the position and specifically stated in the job description such as "must be able to lift 60 pounds without a winch"). Then evaluate her on the basis of her skills and qualifications. You may want to keep looking, however, until you find a candidate whose background and experience more closely meets the requirements of the vacancy than do this candidate's.

Exercise 10

1.	Task-oriented	human relations problems; loner; over-kill on paperwork
2.	Power-oriented	desire for high visibility assignments; manipulation of others (staff) to do the work
3.	Power-oriented	concern about status and reputation; always pushing for more authority
4.	Affiliation-oriented	friendly conversation with co-workers will take precedence over productivity; easily manipulated by his or her overwhelming desire to be liked
5.	Task-oriented	may require a supportive level of supervision because he or she may find it difficult to ask for help if he or she gets in too deeply
6.	Affiliation-oriented	may require close supervision with well-defined goals reviewed weekly; may have difficulty coping with change—any change
7.	Power-oriented	concern about status and reputation; always pushing for more authority; desire for high visibility assignments for which he or she may not be qualified

8.	Task-oriented	human relations problems; loner; he or she may be into being "right" and may be argumentative; may have problems taking responsibility for mistakes
9.	Affiliation-oriented	friendly conversation with co-workers will take precedence over productivity; easily manipulated by his or her overwhelming desire to be liked
10.	Affiliation-oriented	there may be a continuing problem regarding work output, quality, and productivity; he or she may lack good organizational and time-management skills
11.	Power-oriented	manipulator; likes gamesmanship and bargaining; may never work up to his or her full potential
12.	Task-oriented	human relations problems; loner; over-kill on paperwork; not a team player

Exercise 11

Part I

1. listening
2. 20 percent
3. expectations being fulfilled
4. when I first decide I need someone
5. keep silent myself
6. what the right answer is
7. puzzle
8. the primary motivation that drives the candidate's behavior
9. they provide very limited information
10. they provide my selection of possible responses—not the candidate's
11. what they are really feeling; the candidate's honest reaction
12. retain control of the interaction

13. clarifying question

14. repeat the question (use the broken record technique)

15. listening/evaluation

16. a waste of time

17. a dumb strategy

18. I should repeat the question

19. (1) take up time; (2) offer a false choice; (3) ask things for which the answer is obvious; or (4) telegraph the answer the interviewer wants

20. the first 20 minutes

Part II

1. "Please give me an example that illustrates your leadership ability."

2. "Please go on."

3. "Describe a challenging situation you faced and handled as a team leader."

4. "I'm proud to say that in this organization we don't consider age as a factor to anything. All we really look at is a person's skills and experience."

5. "I'd like to hear something about the fires you were putting out."

6. "Sounds like there might be more to it than that."

7. "What specifically would a job have to require of you in order for it to be challenging?"

8. "Give me an example of a situation when that skill was critical to your success."

9. "Absolutely! What other qualities do you think would be important in this job?"

10. "What specific techniques and strategies have you found most useful in directing performance management efforts?"

11. "I'd like to hear about a team project in which you played a team-member role."

12. "Tell me about a situation in which your ability to work well with people was severely challenged."

INTERVIEW QUESTIONS LISTED BY COMPETENCY DESIRED

Adaptable and Flexible

Because every company is continuously changing and growing, you want to hire people who do the same. You need candidates who invite and welcome change, people who understand that change is a part of the everyday life of an organization that believes in continuous improvement. Such people adjust quickly and positively to change. In addition, an adaptable candidate is someone who will show a willingness to take on challenges not specifically within his or her work responsibilities. Here are some questions that may help identify such individuals.

"Please describe a situation that demonstrates your flexibility." *[behavioral question]*

"Tell me about a situation where more responsibility was thrust on you unexpectedly." *[behavioral question]*

"Describe a time when you accepted assistance from someone outside your area on something that was distinctly your personal responsibility." *[behavioral question]*

"What strategies have you used to allow for unexpected changes in your work plans?" *[behavioral question]*

"Describe for me how you have had to reinvent yourself and your skill set in order to meet the company's changing needs." *[behavioral question]*

"What proactive steps have you taken in the past in order to assume broader responsibilities?" *[behavioral question]*

Ambition, Career Goals, and Goal Oriented

In order for the proposed work relationship to be successful, both the company and the candidate must gain support for their respective goals from it. Realize that something the candidate wants very badly is missing in his or her present employment situation because, if he or she were thoroughly and completely satisfied with the present job, he or she wouldn't be sitting in front of you. What is missing that is so critical that the lack of it has driven the candidate to engage in this agonizing activity called job hunting? You want to know what that is. If this vacancy can support and further the candidate's goal and the candidate is qualified for the position, you may have a good match.

"I'd be interested to learn when you last reviewed and updated your long-term career goals. What influenced you to reevaluate them? What specific changes did you make? Why?" *[behavioral question]*

"What standards have you used in the past to measure your personal career success?" *[behavioral question]*

"What would you say is the most important thing you are looking for in a job? How would you know that we could provide you with that?" *[puzzle question]*

"What self-development have you been involved with to prepare yourself for future opportunities? Why those particular activities?" *[behavioral question]*

"What did you hope to find in your previous job that was unavailable and which you hope to find here?" *[puzzle question]*

"If you could write your own job description, what would it contain?" *[puzzle question]*

"What are your long-term career expectations? How does this position fit into those plans?" *[puzzle question]*

"How have you gained support for your goals from previous bosses?" *[behavioral question]*

Analytical Skills and Decision Making

Decision making, the process of making a conscious choice of one alternative from a group of alternatives, is one of the measures of a superior candidate. In today's world, you certainly could not give someone an important job without first considering whether he or she could gather facts, analyze data, and reason things out systematically. The astute candidate knows that decisions cannot be made in a vacuum; attention must be given to how each decision may impact others in the organization. The following questions will assist you in assessing such abilities.

"Would you describe yourself as a logical or intuitive problem solver?" *[puzzle question]*

"Please give me an example from your previous job that illustrates your choice." *[behavioral question]*

"Describe a situation in which you had to be analytical and thorough in making a critical decision. Walk me through the process you followed." *[behavioral question]*

"When you are deciding whether to try something totally new, what weight do you give to the probability of success?" *[puzzle question]*

"What has been the basis on which you determined to take on responsibilities that were not assigned to you or even expected of you?" *[behavioral question]*

"What influenced you to seek a new employment opportunity at this point in your career?" *[behavioral question]*

"Tell me about a decision you made where things did not turn out as well as you had anticipated." *[behavioral question]*

"In retrospect, what should you have done differently?" *[puzzle question]*

Assertive

Assertive behavior is characterized by meticulously clear communication. Others always know exactly what it is the assertive person wants or expects, or where he or she stands on a particular issue. Assertive communication is about setting boundaries and then inviting the other person to participate in negotiating any differences through responsible confrontation. An assertive person is honest, forthright, and not offensive. He or she knows how to be a strong advocate of his or her own ideas, without infringing on the convictions of others. The person accomplishes this in a non-defensive, professional, and unemotional manner that is respectful of others. Here are questions that may help identify such individuals.

"Tell me about a time when you had an idea that you knew would solve a complicated problem and your boss was not interested in hearing about it. What did you do to capture your boss's attention?" *[behavioral question]*

"Describe a situation where you advanced an idea or strategy at a meeting. When your boss and peers heard what you had to say, their reaction was very negative. How did you deal with such a negative onslaught?" *[behavioral question]*

"Tell me about the most challenging confrontational situation you have ever come up against involving a staff member. What made the situation so inflammatory? How did you handle it?" *[behavioral question]*

"Tell me about a time when two of your staff members were locked in a conflict that impacted the entire group. What did you do?" *[behavioral question]*

"On previous jobs, when you discovered organizational practices or procedures that you felt were damaging to employee morale and/or customer satisfaction, what did you do?" *[behavioral question]*

"Tell me about a time when you resolved to pursue a course of action you believed in, despite opposition from others." *[behavioral question]*

Authority, Issues with

You are hiring a person who will be a part of your staff. Although it is important that the candidate be able to work comfortably and cooperatively within the immediate environment, it is essential that he or she be able to get on well with you. Some candidates have a history of authority-based friction; they hate being told what to do. Authority annoys them. Directives rankle them. Rules aggravate them. They may claim that they were just being independent and entrepreneurial and management wanted an automaton. You need some insight as to how the candidate typically handles authority relationships at work.

"Describe a situation where you and your boss disagreed about something you wanted to do. What happened?" *[behavioral question]*

"Tell me about the worst manager you ever had. What made the situation so uncomfortable for you? How did you attempt to deal with it?" *[behavioral question]*

"Tell me about the best manager you ever had. What qualities and techniques did he or she use that you found to be so positive?" *[behavioral question]*

"What part about being managed bothers you the most? Why?" *[puzzle question]*

"What have you found to be the most important factors in establishing and maintaining a good relationship with one's immediate boss?" *[behavioral question]*

"What have been the most serious problems you've had with the people you've worked for? How did you attempt to resolve those issues?" *[behavioral question]*

Beliefs, Values, and Philosophy

Because ultimately people base their decisions on their beliefs, values, and philosophy, the compatibility of these elements with those of the organization becomes a critical factor in the hiring process. An executive who believes that people are disposable and interchangeable will, in the face of downsizing, make different decisions from one who believes that every employee is unique and that those individual differences are the key to the organization's future success. A salesperson who believes that his job is to assist a customer in buying the best product for his or her needs will behave differently from one who believes that her job is to "make my numbers and push product."

"If you were to outline a basic set of values and beliefs upon which to build a sound management philosophy, what factors would you include in it?" *[puzzle question]*

"What has been the most difficult staff decision you have ever had to make? What made that decision so difficult?" *[behavioral question]*

"Tell me about a time when you found that your basic values or beliefs were in conflict with those of the organization. What was the basis of the conflict? How did you attempt to resolve it?" *[behavioral question]*

"Describe for me how some of your daily actions on your previous job were a reflection of your basic beliefs and values." *[behavioral question]*

"In structuring the ideal work environment, what staff behaviors would you encourage; what behaviors would you discourage? Why?" *[puzzle question]*

"What kinds of attitudes in others make you uncomfortable? Why?" *[puzzle question]*

"What kinds of operating principles do you value most (and least) in a work environment?" *[puzzle question]* "Please give me some examples from your previous jobs." *[behavioral question]*

Clerical Skills and Secretarial Candidates

Competent clerical-support persons are often the key to managerial effectiveness. By assuming the bulk of administrative trivia and bureaucratic paperwork, they free their bosses to concentrate on the more critical issues of the business. The primary ingredients to a successful placement depend on (1) skills and (2) personality fit (see page 125) between the assistants and the executives for whom they work so that a highly cohesive partnership can be formed.

"How have you gone about establishing a relationship with a new boss?" *[behavioral question]*

"Tell me about a time when you had to juggle multiple priorities for a number of bosses, all of whom thought their work was the most important and should be done first. How did you sort that out?" *[behavioral question]*

"Please explain how you typically organize your day. What tools and strategies do you like to use?" *[behavioral question]*

"Describe the most difficult boss you've ever worked for and tell me what you did to make your relationship function effectively." *[behavioral question]*

"What kind of people do you find are the most trying in terms of your patience?" *[puzzle question]* "What methods have you used to cope with such individuals?" *[behavioral question]*

"What do you think has been the most valuable contribution you made to your bosses on previous jobs? Why?" *[puzzle question]*

"What system do you typically use for setting priorities? Why? What is your secondary strategy for setting your work priorities?" *[behavioral question]*

Collaborative Relationships

If you are looking for a candidate who will hold a leadership role in your organization, you will need someone with the ability to build and maintain collaborative working relationships. Trust is the essential ingredient in building such relationships. The new hire must be able to generate confidence in his or her brand of leadership by providing each staff member with a sense of stability and consistency. At the same time, this person must advance a sense of mutual accountability and individual responsibility among the staff.

"What strategies have you used to maintain a strong relationship between yourself and each one of your individual staff members?" *[behavioral question]*

"How have you gone about establishing your leadership role with an inherited staff?" *[behavioral question]*

"How have you encouraged individual staff members to freely share information with one another?" *[behavioral question]*

"How often and under what circumstances have you involved the staff in your decision-making and problem-solving efforts?" *[behavioral question]*

"For what purposes would you consider it necessary to get together with peer managers in other areas of the organization?" *[puzzle question]*

"What role have you played in managing conflicts that arise between staff members? Please share with me some specific examples." *[behavioral question]*

"On previous jobs, what issues threatened to damage the cohesiveness of your staff? What strategies did you use to alleviate the threat?" *[behavioral question]*

Communication Skills

The greater the job responsibilities, the more critical it is that the person in that job be a competent communicator. The interview process is a great opportunity to assess a candidate's communication skills. Here you have the chance to evaluate the candidate's ability to express his or her ideas persuasively; describe concepts clearly; organize his or her thoughts sequentially; use appropriate vocabulary and diction; listen and grasp your questions; hold your interest; and maintain good eye contact. The following questions are aimed at testing the candidate's communication skills.

"Describe yourself as you are seen by other people." *[puzzle question]*

"What is it like to work with you?" *[puzzle question]*

"If you were assigned the task of making a presentation to this company's board of directors, what steps would you take to prepare yourself?" *[puzzle question]*

"Tell me about the most challenging communication situation you have ever come up against. What made it challenging?" *[behavioral question]*

"Tell me about a time when you had an idea that would solve a departmental problem. How did you 'sell' the idea to your boss?" *[behavioral question]*

"When you had to give feedback to an employee whose performance had not met expectations, what exactly did you say? What was the impact of your communication?" *[behavioral question]*

Confidence

Confidence is the one attribute that makes a candidate extremely appealing to an interviewer. These are people who demonstrate conviction in their ideas and judgments, confidence in their skills and abilities, and a strong "can-do" belief in themselves to handle any challenge that might come their way. They accept responsibility for the outcomes of their decisions and the results of their actions. In addition, they look at change, conflict, and failure as opportunities for growth.

"What specific qualities make you suitable for this position?" *[puzzle question]*

"Describe an occasion when you stepped beyond the normal bounds of your knowledge and responsibility to take on an unfamiliar task." *[behavioral question]*

"Tell me about a work situation where you faced incredible odds in terms of succeeding but went ahead and tackled the situation anyway. Why did you take on this problem in the first place?" *[behavioral question]*

"What has been the most challenging assignment you have undertaken recently? What made it so challenging? What enabled you to succeed?" *[behavioral question]*

"How do you determine when to take on something risky and when not to do so?" [puzzle question]

"What have you learned about yourself in the past three years?" *[behavioral question]*

"What is the biggest risk you have ever taken at work? What made it risky? What did you do to minimize the risk? How did it turn out?" *[behavioral question]*

Conflict Management and Resolution Skills

Two issues set the stage for work-related conflict: an interdependent relationship between the parties and a deep concern about what is going on. It is a foregone conclusion, therefore, that when people work together, under the pressure of deadlines, conflicting priorities, and division of scarce resources, human relations will become strained. Unless your candidate will be working alone, the issue of conflict-resolution skills becomes vital in evaluating his or her suitability. Typically, the issue surfaces with the closed-ended question, "Do you get along well with other people?" to which the candidate responds, "Yes." What you need to ascertain is whether the candidate manages conflict effectively.

"Describe a situation when you and a peer from another area were in conflict over some interdepartmental issue. How was the problem resolved? What role did you play in its resolution?" *[behavioral question]*

"What experience have you had with conflict-resolution techniques that would enable you to do well in a management role?" *[behavioral question]*

"Tell me about a time when you and your boss didn't agree on how a situation should be handled. How did you resolve your differences?" *[behavioral question]*

"Tell me about an aggravating peer with whom you had to work. What steps did you take to make your relationship somewhat more tolerable?" *[behavioral question]*

"Please describe a common type of conflict situation you experienced in your previous job. What resolution techniques did you use to deal with such situations?" *[behavioral question]*

"What strategies do you most often use in dealing with conflict? Please give me a few examples that illustrate your approach." *[behavioral question]*

Creativity

Creative people are not the easiest to manage. They function as a catalyst, irreverent of consensual views and the customary ways of doing things. They are likely to approach work issues from unexpected angles because they question all the assumptions surrounding a problem. They provide the dynamic that brings about radical change. If your position requires a creative person, look for someone who (1) possesses knowledge, talent, and experience in the field; (2) demonstrates a tolerance for ambiguity and complexity; (3) demonstrates a knowledge of creativity tactics, problem-solving skills, and idea generation; and (4) possesses high energy and an ability for sustained concentration.

"Describe a problem you solved with a exceptionally creative solution." *[behavioral question]*

"How do you balance your reliance on intuition with the facts?" *[puzzle question]*

"Tell me about a time when you tackled a problem for which there was no set procedure, precedent, or historical background. How did you get started?" *[behavioral question]*

"What has been your framework or logic base for tackling an issue that requires an innovative solution?" *[behavioral question]*

"What has been your most creative achievement at work?" *[behavioral question]*

"What types of projects have you been involved with where part of the requirement was innovation?" *[behavioral question]*

"Tell me about the last time you broke the rules." *[behavioral question]*

Creativity, Encourages in Others, and Innovation

Innovation depends not only on hiring creative people but also on managers who know how to build and maintain an environment that nurtures change and risk taking. People with imagination and ingenuity need leadership that understands the needs of the inventive mind and how to inspire it. Such a candidate knows the importance of challenging assignments, open information flow, regular feedback, and clear goals and expectations. Such a candidate is not afraid to allow his or her staff a good deal of autonomy, competent technical support, protection from bureaucratic management directives, and a share in any decision making.

"What methods have you used to encourage risk taking among your people?" *[behavioral question]*

"How you have rewarded risk takers whose results were dubious versus those risk takers whose results were successful?" *[behavioral question]*

"What kinds of things tend to kill a person's creative energy?" *[puzzle question]*

"What methods have you used to structure a working environment for a staff whose central mission was to innovate?" *[behavioral question]*

"What are the differences between managing people whose job involves creativity and managing those whose work is more conventional?" *[puzzle question]*

"In what way does your management style promote creativity?" *[puzzle question]*

"What steps would you take to make sure that a staff of creative people produced what was expected within the designated time frame?" *[puzzle question]*

Customer Service Orientation

A service provider needs an attitude that is not tied to being "right" in every situation. Candidates interested in providing superior customer service to both internal and external clients must be able to identify and understand the needs of others. They must strive to surpass the expectations of their clients. They realize that, without customers, there is no business and that, without an adequate level of service, the customer will not return. They can differentiate the fine line between extraordinary customer service, resulting in a delighted client, and maintaining a healthy business (not giving the store away).

"Please describe a situation in which you were able to turn a negative customer around. What was the issue? How did you accomplish the turn-around?" *[behavioral question]*

"Tell me about a time when you made a personal sacrifice in order to help another person attain a work-related objective." *[behavioral question]*

"What do you think is the difference between quality and customer service?" *[puzzle question]*

"Most customer-service efforts focus on handling complaints. What problems do you see with such a strategy?" *[puzzle question]*

"Describe a situation when the customer's perception of what occurred was clearly wrong. How did you go about resolving the problem?" *[behavioral question]*

"What is an acceptable level of customer dissatisfaction?" *[puzzle question]*

"What strategies have you used for dealing with angry and verbally abusive customers? How have you prevented the aftermath of such an interaction from influencing succeeding interactions?" *[behavioral question]*

Delegation Effectiveness

If the organization is to survive and grow, current leadership must be willing and able to develop staff members so that there is a trained cadre of people available who can eventually move into leadership roles. This means hiring people into leadership positions who know how to (1) encourage the maximum contribution possible from each staff member; (2) inspire and coach people to fulfill and then exceed their individual potential; and (3) nurture and reward responsible risk taking. For a growing organization, this may well be the most critical competency to look for.

"What are the five adjectives that best describe the type of person you have tried to hire? Why have you placed so much value on those particular qualities?" *[behavioral question]*

"What strategies have you used to ensure that one of your people is prepared to assume your current job should you decide to leave?" *[behavioral question]*

"What has happened to those who left your supervision?" *[puzzle question]*

"Quantify your results as a manager who develops others." *[puzzle question]*

"What have you done recently to help individual staff members to become more effective in their present positions? Give me some examples of the kind of assistance you have provided to employees with serious performance problems." *[behavioral question]*

"How have you determined which tasks are delegated to whom? How do you monitor the progress of tasks you have delegated?" *[behavioral question]*

Emotional Maturity, Professionalism, and Stress, Ability to Handle

Emotional maturity is about self-control and not being victimized by one's impulses. Since stress is a common occurrence at work, you want a candidate who has enough self-restraint so that he or she behaves professionally and rationally no matter how upset he or she may be (composure under fire). Being able to repress those impulsive moments of rage and anger should be an essential requirement for anyone going into a leadership role. For those in a customer service position, the skill of maintaining emotional balance with appropriate responses and civility to others who are raging may mean the difference between business lost or gained.

"Describe a situation when your skills in diplomacy and patience were put to the test." *[behavioral question]*

"Tell me about a few situations that created high levels of stress for you at work. What strategies did you use to deal with such occurrences?" *[behavioral question]*

"What strategies have you used to avoid feeling burned out or overwhelmed?" *[behavioral question]*

"How would you evaluate your tolerance for significant and unrealistic pressure from senior management?" *[puzzle question]* "Please give me some examples of how you managed the problems thus created." *[behavioral question]*

"Tell me about a time when one of your staff did something so outrageous and appalling that you wanted to kill him or her on the spot." *[behavioral question]*

"When was the last time you got into an argument at work? What happened? What was the issue involved? How were things resolved?" *[behavioral question]*

Goal Setting

The competent management/supervisory candidate understands that goal setting is a potent leadership strategy. Goal setting provides the manager with a formidable vehicle for controlling the activities of those who report to him or her. Goal setting also moves an employee to higher levels of competence. It is the key ingredient for empowering a person to direct his or her own career. The clearer the notion the employee has about what he or she needs to accomplish, the greater are the chances that it will happen. Having a clear end result in mind is not enough, however. The employee must be able to gauge progress toward that end result. This is achieved by including measurement markers (milestones) along the way. This is what will maintain the employee's motivation.

"What role, if any, have goals and goal setting played in your management strategy? Why? Please give me some examples." *[behavioral question]*

"Tell me about the process you have used to establish your department's goals." *[behavioral question]*

"Please describe the role you have played in the development of your staff members' individual goals." *[behavioral question]*

"How have you motivated your staff to achieve their goals?" *[behavioral question]*

"Describe for me the process you have used for reviewing an employee's progress toward the achievement of his or her individual goals. I'd be interested in learning how often you reviewed progress and about any special techniques you initiated." *[behavioral question]*

"Describe a situation when you had an employee who set easily achievable goals. How did you influence the person to set more challenging goals?" *[behavioral question]*

Individual Contributor (Works Alone/Independently)

There is a category of jobs that require specific knowledge, skills, technical education, and self-supervision. Such jobs do not involve supervision of other people. For this type of job, you want a person who is more comfortable working alone than as part of a team. You need someone who functions independently but who also knows when to seek assistance from others. Such candidates are distinguished by their intensity and drive. They like an environment that values challenging work and rewards achievement. Here are some questions for discovering this type of candidate.

"How do you know when you've done a good job?" *[puzzle question]*

"What kinds of things make your work difficult?" *[behavioral question]*

"Describe for me the type of environment that best nurtures you." *[puzzle question]*

"How do you like to be managed?" *[puzzle question]*

"What aspects of your work have provided you with the most personal satisfaction and enthusiasm? Please give me some examples." *[behavioral question]*

"What kinds of things have created stress and tension that you would like to avoid in future jobs?" *[puzzle question]* "Give me some examples of how you coped with those situations." *[behavioral question]*

"Suppose you were stuck on some portion of a problem. How would you make the judgment as to when someone else's input might be necessary?" *[puzzle question]*

Influences Others and Persuasive

It's easy to persuade others when you are in charge; the difficult task is to influence others when you are not in control. Such an ability requires a talent for building relationships by appealing to common goals and values. It requires a knowledge of the currencies of influence that are typically valued in organizations such as information, contacts, visibility, support, and so on. Candidates who possess the ability to influence others are able to induce co-workers, bosses, and clients to support their ideas and objectives.

"Describe a time when you succeeded in getting someone to go along with something he or she was strongly opposed to doing." *[behavioral question]*

"Tell me about an occasion when you captured the involvement and participation of others to work on and achieve a particular goal. What strategies did you use to accomplish this?" *[behavioral question]*

"Tell me about a time when management was planning to make a change that would have a detrimental effect on your job. What steps did you take to influence management that the change should NOT be made? Why do you think your efforts were successful (or not successful)?" *[behavioral question]*

"Describe a time when you worked for a manager who assigned work at the last possible minute. What attempts did you make to influence a change in that manager's modus operandi?" *[behavioral question]*

"Tell me how you influenced a staff member to assume more responsibility or to take on a task that you knew would be difficult." *[behavioral question]*

"Describe a situation when you had to influence someone higher up in the organization who had a reputation for being hard-headed. What was your strategy?" *[behavioral question]*

"Suppose I told you that you are one of three excellent candidates for this position. How would you convince me that you are the one I should hire?" *[puzzle question]*

Initiative Taking and Enterprising

An important attribute to look for in candidates is that of initiative taking. This quality is prized because such a person is (1) willing to go beyond the boundaries of the specific job responsibilities; (2) able to work with minimal supervision; and (3) always searching for better ways of doing things (an entrepreneurial spirit). In the search for continuous improvement, these people pursue innovative, imaginative projects with energy and enthusiasm. Although such projects can contribute to an organization's long-term success by helping to keep it ahead of the curve, they also foster a challenging and chaotic workplace.

"Describe a situation when using your initiative got you into trouble." *[behavioral question]*

"Tell me about the last time you pushed for more responsibility and found yourself in over your head. How did you rescue the situation?" *[behavioral question]*

"Relate an incident where you secured resources that were difficult to obtain but which were necessary in order for you to achieve a goal." *[behavioral question]*

"On previous jobs, what organizational problems did you try to solve that were not specifically related to your job responsibilities?" *[behavioral question]*

"What changes in your job have you made over the past three months? Why did you focus on those particular areas? How did you ensure the changes would work?" *[behavioral question]*

"In a new job, how would you determine whether changes needed to be made? How would you introduce your ideas for change?" *[puzzle question]*

Integrity Driven

Integrity is not something you teach an adult. It becomes an integral part of an individual's makeup at a very early age and permeates every decision and action. People with integrity act from a strong moral base. When the work involves handling other people's money, organizations are careful to select candidates who conduct themselves with honesty and integrity in both their business and personal activities. An employee with integrity does not play *with* the rules, doing things that *might* be considered unethical. You should look for candidates who can be relied on to act in the best interests of customers, co-workers, and the organization. Here are some questions that can help identify such individuals.

"What strategies and techniques have you used in order to keep your integrity clean with regard to your staff?" *[behavioral question]*

"Suppose you knew that people in your area (or your staff) were pilfering office supplies. Would you do anything about it and, if so, what would you do?" *[puzzle question]*

"Tell me about a time when your integrity was challenged by a customer or client. What did you do?" *[behavioral question]*

"Relate a situation from your previous work experience where you were asked to do something you believed would damage your integrity. How did you handle that situation?" *[behavioral question]*

"Salespeople make exaggerated claims about their product's capability. Bosses promise raises knowing that additional funds are not available. Secretaries tell unwelcome callers that the boss is not there when he or she is there. Conventional wisdom tells us that such white lies are a business necessity. What has been your experience with such white lies?" *[behavioral question]*

"In a typical business environment, what situations can you think of where total honesty would be inappropriate?" *[puzzle question]*

Interpersonal Skills

The primary reason people are terminated is their inability to get along with co-workers. In addition, the quality of someone's interpersonal skills plays a crucial role in determining his or her eventual job success. If asked, candidates will claim they have good people skills. It is important to look at two areas: (1) basic attitude toward other people and (2) ability to establish and maintain productive relationships with others whose deficiencies and irritating behavior they acknowledge.

"Give me some examples from previous jobs that illustrate your ability to handle frustrating situations and unreasonable people." *[behavioral question]*

"Tell me about a time when you had to influence someone higher up in the organization who had a reputation for being hard-headed." *[behavioral question]*

"What type of person have you found is most difficult to work with? Why? What have you done in order to work productively with such a person?" *[behavioral question]*

"How do you feel you've been treated by your co-workers over the years?" *[puzzle question]*

"Tell me about a situation when your boss was upset about a decision you had made. How did you handle your boss's anger?" *[behavioral question]*

"Describe a time when a peer made an unjustified complaint about something you did. How did you correct his or her perception of the situation?" *[behavioral question]*

"In giving unpleasant news to a very sensitive, emotional employee, what strategies did you use to keep the conversation on an even keel?" *[behavioral question]*

Leadership Skills

Leadership is about influencing others to achieve organizational goals. It includes a use of power that is not based on domination and an understanding of how one's behavior can impact the staff. An effective leader allows people some autonomy so they can influence the factors that affect their jobs. He or she encourages people to solve their own problems. He or she also provides the staff with (1) a clear sense of direction (goals); (2) an ongoing development process to increase skills; (3) a competent feedback system so people can tell how they are doing; (4) cooperative (not competitive) staff relationships; and (5) conflict resolution through mutual confrontation. He or she also keeps staff focused on continual improvement by encouraging people to set goals for their own growth.

"What have you done to maintain a strong relationship between yourself and each individual staff member?" *[behavioral question]*

"What role do you typically play in managing conflicts that arise between staff members?" *[behavioral question]*

"What techniques have you used to encourage your people to give you the 'bad news' when they screw things up?" *[behavioral question]*

"Please tell me what strategies you have used in order to build and maintain an atmosphere of trust in your department." *[behavioral question]*

"How have you ensured objectivity when evaluating the performance of one of your staff?" *[behavioral question]*

"What techniques have you used to encourage employees to develop their own capabilities?" *[behavioral question]*

"How often and under what circumstances do you involve your staff in your decision-making and problem-solving efforts?" *[behavioral question]*

Management Competence

Managing others requires strong human relations skills, competent organizational skills, and a good deal of old-fashioned common sense. Many people find their way into management roles without any of those things and consequently cause much strife, confusion, and the loss of talented staff. If you are looking for a candidate who will hold a leadership role (supervisor, team leader, lead person), understand that experience as a supervisor does not automatically qualify a candidate as a good leader. The following questions may help your assessment process.

"What strategies have you used to control department operations and monitor staff performance?" *[behavioral question]*

"What process have you used to forecast manpower needs?" *[behavioral question]*

"How have you prepared for and run your staff meetings?" *[behavioral question]*

"How have you determined and then communicated developmental needs to individual staff members?" *[behavioral question]*

"When you had to introduce an unpopular change to your staff, what steps did you take to minimize any negative reactions?" *[behavioral question]*

"When a new employee joins your group, how have you ensured that he or she gets settled in and accepted by the staff quickly?" *[behavioral question]*

"How have you structured opportunities for communication and interaction with your staff and for what purposes?" *[behavioral question]*

Management Style or Operating Style Used

Management style is the consistent pattern of behavior a person exhibits in attempting to influence the activities of others in achieving organizational goals. It is developed over time and is what others recognize as a personal style. Since a good management style in one situation may be a dismal failure in another, a strong candidate for a leadership position would know that there is no such thing as a best all-purpose management style. The most effective leaders are those who can vary their style according to the particular needs of the situation. Power is the hard side of leadership. A good candidate for a leadership role would know that using his or her authority for accomplishment rather than fear and domination is the mark of an effective leader. The following questions will help you assess the candidate's management style.

"How much structure and direction do you typically provide to your staff?" *[behavioral question]*

"Tell me about a leader you admire and after whom you've patterned your own management style." *[behavioral question]*

"Please paint a picture of the type of culture you would want to create here if we hired you. What specific steps would you take to establish that kind of culture?" *[puzzle question]*

"What behaviors and attitudes in your staff members have you consistently encouraged? How?" *[behavioral question]*

"What behaviors and attitudes in your staff members have you consistently attempted to eliminate? How?" *[behavioral question]*

"Under what circumstances have you allowed the staff to determine their own work priorities, activities, and decision making? Under what circumstances have you determined the tasks, procedures, and priorities for the staff?" *[behavioral question]*

Motivation and Drive

A skilled candidate with a keen interest in the particular type of work or who is excited by the industry is far more likely to be a superior performer than is someone who is merely looking for a job. You want someone with a compelling desire to achieve who is constantly working to get better at what he or she does. Such a candidate would have an expanding track record within his or her field of endeavor.

"What turns you on about this kind of work?" *[puzzle question]*

"Describe a situation that illustrates your passion for this kind of work." *[behavioral question]*

"What have you done recently to expand your industry (or technical) knowledge?" *[behavioral question]*

"Tell me about a time when you took on a difficult assignment for its developmental potential. What did you learn?" *[behavioral question]*

"Why do you think this industry (or technology) will continue to hold your interest?" *[puzzle question]*

"What have you done recently to become more effective?" *[behavioral question]*

"How have your career interests changed over the years?" *[behavioral question]*

Organization and Planning Skills

Organization and planning skills have to do with the manager's ability to establish a time management strategy for his or her department—one that guarantees the successful completion of the department's mission. Just as in personal time use, recognition that time is NOT a renewable resource and that effective planning is critical to a successful outcome is what separates the adequate manager from the superior one. In the interview situation, look for the candidate who has formulated some overall strategy for time use.

"Describe the process you use for planning." *[behavioral question]*

"Tell me about a time when planning got in the way of results." *[behavioral question]*

"What methods have you used to establish priorities for your department?" *[behavioral question]*

"What special techniques have you used to manage the work week of your staff so that both realistic deadlines and unexpected crisis were appropriately handled?" *[behavioral question]*

"How have you encouraged your staff to organize and plan their work?" *[behavioral question]*

"What tools have you used for organizing the work flow in your department?" *[behavioral question]*

"How far in advance have you made your planning decisions? At what point do you inform the staff of your plans or bring them into the process?" *[behavioral question]*

"Conventional wisdom claims that planning avoids the fire-fighting syndrome. Give me an example that proves or disproves this for you." *[behavioral question]*

Persistence

Assessing how candidates will respond to difficult times is quite different from determining how they react when everything is going smoothly. Sadly, the true measure of a candidate may not become evident until he or she is actually on the job and confronting a major road block. You want a person who, when confronted with obstacles, will keep going regardless of how difficult the situation may be. Such people are resolute about completing whatever they start and tenacious in achieving their goals despite any difficulties involved.

"Tell me about a time when you knew you were right but that the odds of winning others to your point of view were slim. How long did you fight before abandoning your position? What told you it was time to give up?" *[behavioral question]*

"Tell me about a time when you feel you gave up too soon." *[behavioral question]*

"Give me an example of your perseverance in the face of tremendous odds." *[behavioral question]*

"Describe how you keep yourself enthusiastic and motivated on long-term projects where success and completion may be years of hard effort away." *[behavioral question]*

"What specific hurdles have you overcome in your career to get where you are today?" *[behavioral question]*

"Describe a time when you were criticized for being stubborn or inflexible and explain why this complaint may have occurred." *[behavioral question]*

"What has been the most difficult project for you to see through to the end? What made completion so difficult?" *[behavioral question]*

"Give me an example of how you went that extra mile on an assignment to ensure that all necessary bases were covered." *[behavioral question]*

Personality Fit

Open-ended and minimally structured questions may be used to prompt a candidate into revealing which of three primary motivational drives propels most of his or her behavior. Here are seven such questions with an indication of the likely responses from each of the three types of candidates.

1. "Tell me about your most recent job."

task-oriented candidate:	prioritized or chronological list of job activities
affiliation-oriented candidate:	description of the personalities of co-workers
power-oriented candidate:	control of; in charge of; job title

2. "What kinds of things make your work difficult?"

task-oriented candidate:	other people who are stupid, slow, or won't listen
affiliation-oriented candidate:	being overworked; long hours; working alone
power-oriented candidate:	being over-supervised; too much red tape

3. "What do you consider your greatest strengths to be?"

task-oriented candidate:	hard worker; dedicated to excellence
affiliation-oriented candidate:	getting along well with other people
power-oriented candidate:	able to take charge; to influence others

4. "Why does this job interest you?"

task-oriented candidate:	challenge; something new; opportunity to learn
affiliation-oriented candidate:	near my home; I've done it before; friends work here
power-oriented candidate:	represents advancement; good career move

5. "Give me an example of a difficult problem you solved or decision you had to make."

    task-oriented candidate: describes a technical problem

    affiliation-oriented candidate: describes an interpersonal problem

    power-oriented candidate: describes some political intrigue or power maneuver

6. "What are the most important qualities I should look for in a person to do this type of work?" (The candidate will describe him- or herself)

    task-oriented candidate: dependable; hard-working; honest

    affiliation-oriented candidate: helpful; friendly; cooperative; likes people

    power-oriented candidate: has leadership potential; wants to move up

7. "What do you do in your spare time?"

    task-oriented candidate: competitive non-team activities (tennis); attends night school; reads; surfs the Internet

    affiliation-oriented candidate: participates in team sports, spectator sports; member of support groups and social groups

    power-oriented candidate: interested in politics, world affairs; leader of a team, group, or club; interested in investments and money

Recent Graduate and Inexperienced Candidate

When looking at recent graduates (candidates with little or no work experience), you hope to find a person with the ability to learn quickly and the potential to grow into a leadership position. You want a candidate who already exhibits some decision-making ability, who realizes the importance of perseverance (time + effort = results), and who possesses some level of insight about people. The following questions target those issues.

"Which of the part-time jobs you held while in school/college did you find most interesting? Why?" *[behavioral question]*

"What were your most and least favorite courses? Why?" *[behavioral question]*

"What subjects did you do best in? What subjects did you not handle as well as you would have liked? What, if anything, did you do to strengthen your proficiency in those subjects?" *[behavioral question]*

"What was the most challenging situation you faced in school/college? Why?" *[behavioral question]*

"What was the most rewarding experience? Why?" *[behavioral question]*

"How did you choose the extracurricular activities in which you took part? What did you learn about yourself from engaging in those activities?" *[behavioral question]*

"What have you done in school that would illustrate initiative?" *[behavioral question]*

"Tell me about a time when your academic requirements came into conflict with other activities or interests. How did you resolve the conflict?" *[behavioral question]*

Salesmanship (Ability to Sell)

The most complicated position of all is that of salesperson. Perhaps it is because customers must first "buy" the salesperson before they can purchase the product or service. Maybe it's because a good salesperson needs to possess so many contradictory abilities: (1) listening and speaking skills; (2) product knowledge and people savvy; (3) selling acumen and market penetration strategies; (4) compelling but non-manipulative communication skills; (5) motivation to achieve high levels of individual performance along with a desire to serve the customer; (6) aggressive yet personable; (7) dedicated to success yet resilient in the face of rejection; and (8) a self-starter who enjoys interacting with others. Here are some questions to help assess sales candidates.

"What do you know about our product line and about our customer base?" *[puzzle question]*

"What are the three primary reasons someone might purchase our products?" *[puzzle question]*

"What trends do you see in this industry that might affect this company and our products?" *[puzzle question]*

"Walk me through the typical selling strategy you used with a new customer in your previous job." *[behavioral question]*

"Sell me this pen." *[behavioral question]*

"Describe how you influenced a customer to purchase your higher priced product when he or she had been buying a competitor's similar, lower priced product." *[behavioral question]*

"How many hours per week have you found it necessary to work in order to get the job done at a level that meets your satisfaction?" *[behavioral question]*

"How have you dealt with customer procrastination or decision reluctance?" *[behavioral question]*

"If you were developing a 'salesmanship' course for new recruits, what topics would you include? Why?" *[puzzle question]*

Self-Appraisal Questions

Questions of this type ask candidates to analyze their behavior, experiences, and skills from their own point of view. They provide an opportunity to discover what the candidate thinks of him- or herself. In addition, these questions can yield some insight into the candidate's self-image, level of self-esteem, self-awareness, and self-knowledge.

"What do you consider your greatest strengths to be?" *[puzzle question]*

"What would your previous bosses say were the major factors or qualities that made you especially valuable to them?" *[puzzle question]*

"If you were sitting in my chair interviewing you, what would be your greatest concern regarding your overall qualifications for this position?" *[puzzle question]*

"How do you evaluate your own performance?" *[puzzle question]*

"When others describe you, what qualities do they mention first?" *[puzzle question]*

"If hired, what would you contribute to this job that other candidates could not?" *[puzzle question]*

"Why do you feel you would be good for this position?" *[puzzle question]*

Self-Development

Today, with such fast technological changes, a person's skills can rapidly become obsolete. A good candidate for ANY job is one who makes an effort to keep his or her knowledge current. Self-development is something a person does for him- or herself, not because the boss or the organization requires it. It is done because the individual is motivated by a desire to improve. During the interview, listen also for situations in which learning was possible if the candidate accepted responsibility for errors he or she had made in judgment or actions (learning from the experience). Here are some questions that may shed some light on this area.

"Tell me about learning something new about yourself in the course of a project or assignment." *[behavioral question]*

"What circumstances or events influenced you to learn something totally new? How did you go about acquiring that new knowledge or skill?" *[behavioral question]*

"What reading do you do that is related to your work? Please summarize what you have learned over the past six months from your research." *[behavioral question]*

"Over the past twelve months, how much of your own time and/or money have you invested in your own personal development and for what specific purposes?" *[behavioral question]*

"What strategies have you used to purposefully strengthen your skills and knowledge on the job?" *[behavioral question]*

"Tell me about an important learning that came about as the result of a mistake or failure. How have you used that learning in other situations?" *[behavioral question]*

Self-Starter, Independent Thinker, and Works Without Supervision

The qualities of self-motivation and self-governance are critical in candidates. Such people can function with a minimum of supervision and structure. They can be relied on to figure out what needs to be done and, without someone or something to nudge them along, will move ahead and get it done. Such people are sometimes referred to as self-starters or independent thinkers because they can work effectively on their own.

"Describe a situation when you were forced to make a decision that was outside the normal limits of your knowledge, experience, and authority." *[behavioral question]*

"Give me an example of how you have had to reinvent yourself or redefine your responsibilities to meet the company's changing needs." *[behavioral question]*

"Tell me about any higher level responsibilities you assumed on your own in your previous job. How did those opportunities come about?" *[behavioral question]*

"What typically gives you the most satisfaction in a job?" *[puzzle question]*

"Tell me about the last time you broke the rules." *[behavioral question]*

"What changes have occurred in your last job because of you?" *[behavioral question]*

"Tell me about the biggest career risk you have ever taken." *[behavioral question]*

"Describe a situation when you took action without getting approval first." *[behavioral question]*

Selling the Job

The ideal candidate is seated before you (he or she has the right background, education, training, and attitude). Now you must entice the candidate to join your company. Do not start by explaining how great the organization is and what a terrific career opportunity this position is without first discovering what it is that the candidate wants. Unless you find out first what the candidate is looking for, there is no way you can sell the candidate on joining your organization. (Remember: If your organization cannot provide whatever the candidate deems to be important and you convince him or her to join the organization anyway, you have guaranteed a turnover statistic.)

"If you could construct this job exactly the way you would want it, what would it look like?" *[puzzle question]*

"What would convince you that we have the ideal job for you?" *[puzzle question]*

"What would have to change at your present position in order for you to continue working there?" *[puzzle question]*

"What are the critical factors a job must have in order to satisfy you?" *[puzzle question]*

"What would it look like to you if this organization could offer you that kind of challenge [or responsibility or whatever it is that the candidate says he or she wants]?" *[puzzle question]*

"What do you hope to find here that you haven't found at your previous job?" *[puzzle question]*

"What has gotten in the way of other jobs being able to give you these things?" *[puzzle question]*

"What efforts did you make to initiate those opportunities for yourself at other jobs?" *[behavioral question]*

Strategist (Sees the Big Picture), Risk Taker, Political Astuteness

Candidates who are good strategists never lose sight of the larger objectives associated with their jobs and the organization's fundamental position in the marketplace. They identify complex situations and seek solutions that advance the organization's primary goals (such as increasing quality service, expanding growth, and improving profitability). Such individuals are politically astute in conflict situations; they are quick to identify common areas of agreement when controversies occur over such things as priorities and division of scarce resources. They are also sensitive to the political issues within an organization and calibrate their decision making accordingly. This type of candidate would come to the interview armed with some knowledge of the industry and the major issues confronting the organization in the marketplace.

"Tell me about a time when you identified a fundamental problem underlying your organization's policy and/or practice. What did you prescribe as a more effective approach?" *[behavioral question]*

"In the past, when you were faced with making a politically risky decision, what factors did you consider before moving ahead?" *[behavioral question]*

"When you are making decisions, how do you go about determining how those decisions will impact other parts of the organization?" *[behavioral question]*

"What are the critical issues that might confront this industry in the next ten years? How are you preparing yourself to deal with those changes?" *[puzzle question]*

"What was the basis on which you decided to take on tasks, projects, or responsibilities that were not assigned or expected of you?" *[behavioral question]*

"In your last job, what kind of outside influences tended to shape internal policy? What kind of impact did this have on you and on your job?" *[behavioral question]*

Team Player

Experience on a team does not automatically qualify a candidate as a good team player. Working in a team setting requires strong human relations skills, some knowledge of negotiation techniques, a willingness to compromise, and a resolve to put team goals ahead of one's personal agenda. Many people find their way onto teams totally devoid of all those prerequisites. As a result, they cause problems that negatively affect the group's productivity. You want a person who can work cooperatively and collaboratively with peers—someone who understands that a team's human relations process is every bit as important as the team's mission.

"What has been the most valuable piece of learning you gained from participating in a team effort? How have you used that learning in succeeding situations?" *[behavioral question]*

"What specific difficulties have you found to be fairly common in all the team experiences you've had?" *[behavioral question]*

"Describe a situation when you were a member of a team that had to set its own performance parameters. What role did you play in the process?" *[behavioral question]*

"As a team member, how have leadership issues usually been resolved?" *[behavioral question]*

"What has been your experience with conflict resolution in a team setting where outside intervention was not utilized?" *[behavioral question]*

"What do you like most/least about working in a team setting?" *[behavioral question]*

"Describe for me the circumstances under which you have worked most effectively on a team." *[behavioral question]*

Time Management

Effective utilization of time separates the adequate employee or manager from the superior one. You want a candidate who knows how to manage him- or herself so that he or she makes maximum use of this critical, inflexible, non-renewable resource. Such a person will have formulated some overall strategy for time use that is designed to (1) expand his or her productivity by evaluating priorities and (2) develop techniques that effectively identify and control those things that waste time.

"Time management is really all about managing oneself. What evidence can you point to that proves you manage your time well?" *[behavioral question]*

"What new ideas or strategies have you put in place that are designed to save time?" *[behavioral question]*

"Think of the five major components of your previous job. How did you determine how much time to spend on each?" *[behavioral question]*

"What do you think is the most significant piece of information regarding time management that a person ought to understand?" *[puzzle question]*

"What strategies have you used for dealing with interruptions?" *[behavioral question]*

"How have you dealt with someone who left his or her work (or who assigned you work) for the very last possible minute?" *[behavioral question]*

"What has been the most critical time management issue you faced in a job? How did you overcome the difficulty?" *[behavioral question]*

Versatility

Versatile describes someone who is able to assume a large assortment of different responsibilities because he or she has talent, skills, knowledge, or ability in a number of different areas. Versatile also refers to someone who knows how to alter his or her operating style in order to achieve organizational goals or to gain cooperation from others.

"Tell me about the variety of assignments with which you were involved on your previous job and whether these assignments were sequential or simultaneous." *[behavioral question]*

"Describe a situation where you modified your customary behavioral style so that you could work effectively with a person whom you did not like." *[behavioral question]*

"Describe an occasion when you had to juggle multiple priorities from different areas of the business." *[behavioral question]*

"Describe for me how you have had to reinvent yourself and your skill set in order to meet the company's changing needs." *[behavioral question]*

"Tell me about any proactive steps you have taken in the past in order to assume broader responsibilities outside your area of expertise." *[behavioral question]*

"What were the tasks or assignments in your last job that allowed you to try out new ways of doing things or required that you come up with innovative ideas?" *[behavioral question]*

"What kinds of challenges have you faced in your career that compelled you to look at other disciplines or fields for the solutions?" *[behavioral question]*

Why the Candidate Is Making a Job Change

Most candidates will paint a rosy picture regarding their skills, values, and abilities. You find yourself wondering, "If this person is so fantastic, how come the current employer doesn't see that?" The candidate assures you that he or she is not being forced out by the present employer due to poor performance or economic belt-tightening; he or she has made the decision to leave. The assumption, then, is that the present job is somehow no longer meeting this person's needs or goals. In order to properly assess the candidate's suitability for your job, you must find out what his or her goals are and then decide whether your position will satisfy those goals.

"What are some of the reasons why you are considering leaving your present job?" *[puzzle question]*

"Under what circumstances would you remain at your present job?" *[puzzle question]*

"What has been the major contributing factor that convinced you your present position no longer held any promise or potential for you?" *[behavioral question]*

"Tell me about the specific events or incidents that contributed the most to your decision to seek another employment position." *[behavioral question]*

"What do you hope to find here that you haven't been able to find at your present job?" *[puzzle question]*

"Please describe the difference between what your present job offers you and what you would like your ideal job to offer you. Why is it important for you to have those things in a job?" *[puzzle question]*

Work Environment Preferred; Job Satisfaction, Assessing What Contributes to, and Management Style of Boss Preferred

Something the candidate wants very badly is missing in his or her present employment situation. If he or she were completely satisfied with the current employment situation, he or she would not be sitting in front of you. In order to make sure there is a good fit between the candidate and your organization, you need to know what the candidate thinks is missing from his or her current employment situation. Perhaps the candidate does not like the way he or she is being managed. Maybe the tasks are no longer fulfilling or challenging. Perhaps the environment is no longer conducive or comfortable for sustained effort. You need to obtain a clear picture of the environment in which the candidate feels fulfilled.

"What factors have the most influence on your level of job satisfaction?" *[puzzle question]*

"Describe what would be the ideal work environment for you." *[puzzle question]*

"From the standpoint of job responsibilities, which of your past positions did you find most fulfilling? Why?" *[behavioral question]*

"Which did you find least fulfilling? Why?" *[behavioral question]*

"Please describe the work environment in which you believe you did your best work. What variables contributed most to your sense of accomplishment?" *[behavioral question]*

"Describe the best job you ever had. What made it the best?" *[behavioral question]*

"Tell me about the worst manager you ever had. I'd be interested in learning what made the situation especially uncomfortable for you." *[behavioral question]*

"Tell me about the best manager you ever had. What were the qualities and techniques he or she used that you found to be personally beneficial?" *[behavioral question]*

RESOURCES

Basic Interviewing Skills

Adams, B., & Veruki, P. (1997). *Hiring top performers.* Holbrook, MA: Adams Media.

Beatty, R. (1994). *Interviewing and selecting high performers.* New York: John Wiley & Sons.

Deems, R. (1995). *Hiring: More than a gut feeling.* Franklin Lakes, NJ: Career Press.

Falcone, P. (1997). *96 great interview questions to ask before you hire.* New York: AMACOM.

Famularo, J. (Ed.). (1972). *Handbook of modern personnel administration.* New York: McGraw-Hill.

Half, R. (1986). *Robert Half on hiring.* New York: New American Library.

Jenks, J. (1996). *Hiring, firing (and everything in between) personnel forms book.* Ridgefield, CT: Round Lake Publishing.

Marvin, P. (1973). *The right man for the right job.* Homewood, IL: Dow-Jones-Irwin.

Mercer, M. (1993). *Hire the best and avoid the rest.* New York: AMACOM.

Messmer, M. (1998). *Fast forward MBA in hiring.* New York: John Wiley & Sons.

Pinsker, R. (1991). *Hiring winners.* New York: AMACOM.

Yate, M. (1988). *Hiring the best.* Holbrook, MA: Bob Adams.

Body Language

Ball, P. (1996). *Straight talk is more than words.* Grahamville, OH: Knox.

Birdwhistell, R. (1970). *Kinesis and context: Essays on body motion communication.* Philadelphia, PA: University of Pennsylvania Press.

Dimitrus, J.E., & Mazzarella, M. (1998). *Reading people.* New York: Random House.

Fast, J. (1974). *Body language.* New York: Penguin Books.

Mehrabian, A. (1971). *Silent messages.* Belmont, CA: Wadsworth.

Nierenberg, G., & Calero, H. (1971). *How to read a person like a book.* New York: Hawthorn Books.

Legal Considerations, Restrictions, and Issues

Olsen, W.J. (1997). *The excuse factory: How employment law is paralyzing the American workplace.* New York: Free Press.

Roberson, C. (1992). *Hire right, fire right.* New York: McGraw-Hill.

Rogers, J., & Fortson, W. (1976). *Fair employment interviewing.* Reading, MA: Addison-Wesley.

Sweet, D. (1998). *The modern employment function.* Reading, MA: Addison-Wesley

Sovereign, K. (1998). *Personnel law.* Englewood Cliffs, NJ: Prentice Hall.

Listening Skills

Bandler, R., & Grinder, J. (1979). *Frogs into princes.* Moab, UT: Real People Press.

Dugger, J. (1995). *Listen up: Hear what's really being said.* National Press Publications.

Friedman, P. (1987). *Listening processes: Attention, understanding and evaluation.* New York: AMACOM.

Montgomery, R. (1981). *Listening made easy.* New York: AMACOM.

O'Connor, J., & Seymour, J. (1993). *Introducing neuro-linguistic programming.* London: Aquarian Press.

Psychological Background

Goleman, D. (1995). *Emotional intelligence.* New York: Bantam.

McClelland, D. (1968). *The achieving society.* New York: Van Nostrand Reinhold.

Seligman, M. (1993). *What you can change and what you can't.* New York: Knopf.

Smart, B. (1983). *Selection interviewing.* New York: John Wiley & Sons.

Sternberg, R. (1996). *Successful intelligence.* New York: Simon & Schuster.